BIRDS

OF THE

AMERICAN SOUTHWEST

BIRDS

OF THE

AMERICAN SOUTHWEST

LYNN HASSLER

RIO NUEVO PUBLISHERS
TUCSON, ARIZONA

INTRODUCTION

· · · · · ·

IF BIRDS INTRIGUE YOU, YOU'RE NOT ALONE. Birdwatching is among the fastest-growing outdoor pastimes in the United States and is enjoyed by millions of people. It's possible to see birds practically anywhere, and they are the most conspicuous and dynamic form of wildlife that most of us experience.

Throughout the ages, flight has been a source of wonder. We marvel at the ability of birds to fly with grace and ease, and the notion of taking wing and flying far and wide appeals to the wanderlust in many of us. Bird migration, even after decades of research, continues to hold many mysteries. What causes birds to follow certain flyways and routes between their summer and winter homes? How can a tiny hummingbird find its way as it travels thousands of miles in spring and fall?

Many birds are feathered with eye-catching, brilliant colors that appeal to our sense of beauty. Of course, feathers do more for the birds than give them visual appeal. They enable flight, they insulate and waterproof, and they provide streamlining and camouflage.

Birds have intricate and fascinating behavior patterns. Some hover at flowers, some run on the ground, some climb trees, and others soar to great heights. Many are quite specialized in their diets, while others eat whatever comes their way. Some birds have bizarre courtship rituals. Some build elaborate nests, others build no nest at all, and a few don't even raise their own young.

Many species have melodic songs that provide pleasing music for the outdoors. Some birds warble, others squawk, and still others imitate a wide variety of sounds. Of course, not all birds are beautiful to look at, and not all of them have musical songs. Some of the oddest-looking and least melodious birds are among the most captivating.

About This Book

The purpose of this book is to introduce you to some of the most significant birds of the American Southwest. It is not intended to be a comprehensive field guide, but it does include essential information on identification for 109 species. The photographs serve to give a general idea of these birds' appearance and will help you recognize them in the field. This book also describes important behaviors characteristic to each bird. You may be astonished to learn some of the things that these birds do for a living.

Birds become more interesting to us when we know something about them and when we know their names. Fortunately, unlike the situation in the plant world (where there are multiple common names for each species), the English names for birds are quite standardized. It is not necessary to learn their scientific names to communicate about them. Scientific names of the birds and their families are included here, however, and these sometimes provide interesting sidelights of their own. In addition, Spanish names are given, although use may vary by location.

Approximate sizes are given in inches. Lengths are measured from the tip of the bill to the end of the tail. In some cases a range of sizes is given—generally due to differences in measurements between males and females. Wingspans are also provided. It should be noted that these are average approximations, taken from a number of different published works, and that individual variations always occur.

For the purposes of this book, the region defined as the Southwest ranges from southeastern California through Arizona, New Mexico, and into western Texas and northern Mexico, and includes adjacent areas of Nevada, Utah, and southwest Colorado. This is an area that is very rich in bird life, with more than four hundred species residing here or visiting every year. Species selected for inclusion in this book are common and/or conspicuous in the Southwest, either as part-time or permanent residents.

A few Southwestern specialty birds, which occur only in this region of North America, also are included.

Many people think of the Southwest as a hot, desert region. The desert is fascinating in its own right, but this habitat is found mainly at the lowest elevations in the area. As a general rule, average temperatures decrease and the amount of annual rainfall increases as you ascend from the desert floor through the foothills and into the mountains of the Southwest. At some middle elevations, there are sweeping grasslands that rival those of the Great Plains. In others, there are open woodlands of piñon pine and juniper. Extensive woodlands of oak are typical of the foothills and mountain slopes in many areas. High in the mountains, there are cooler zones with pine, spruce, and Douglas fir trees. At all elevations, the edges of streams and ponds support different trees and shrubs. Each of these habitats has its own distinct set of birds and other wildlife. This range in elevation is found over much of the West, but the Southwest has the added feature of many subtropical species that spill across the border from Mexico.

Just as the bird life changes as you transition from one habitat to another, the cast of characters also changes with the seasons. Be prepared to see different birds at different times of year. No two birds have exactly the same requirements for living. Many are permanent residents, here all year. Some arrive to nest and raise their young in the spring and summer, and others spend only winters in the Southwest. Still others come through in migration, stopping for food and shelter on their way elsewhere.

Birdwatching, or birding, can be whatever you want it to be: a casual activity done from your kitchen window; an intellectual game in which you see how many kinds of birds you can identify; an excuse for traveling to a variety of habitats; a relaxing way to enjoy the out-of-doors and escape the stresses of everyday life; or, quite simply, a way to have fun. Whatever your reason, we hope that this book will enhance your enjoyment of nature's winged creatures, and that it will lead you to a deeper respect for the natural world.

SPECIES ACCOUNTS

· · · · · ·

SPECIES IN THIS BOOK ARE ARRANGED IN TAXONOMIC ORDER. That is, species are placed in the sequence of their presumed natural relationships. The birds that are thought to be the most primitive are covered first, proceeding on a continuum to the most highly evolved species. Taxonomists do not always agree, and so this order is subject to change. The sequence for this book is based on the classification approved by the American Ornithologists' Union (A.O.U.) current at the time of publication: *The A.O.U. Check-list of North American Birds, Seventh Edition.*

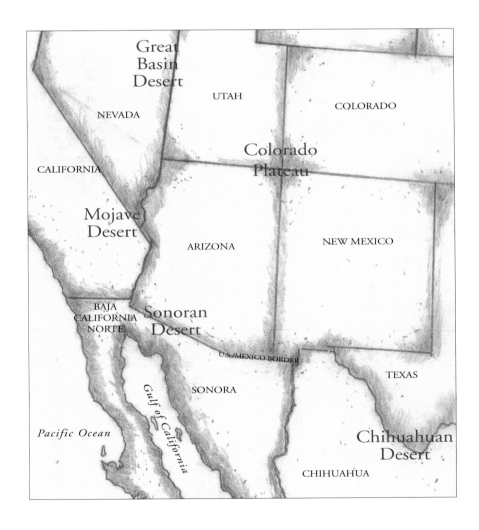

Black-bellied Whistling-Duck

Dendrocygna autumnalis

SPANISH: *Pijije de ala blanca*

FAMILY: Ducks, Geese, and Swans–Anatidae

LENGTH & WINGSPAN: 21 inches; 30 inches

With their upright bearing and longish legs, black-bellied whistling-ducks are almost goose-like in appearance. Often seen striding about in flooded agricultural fields or near ponds, these comely creatures feed on grasses, waste grains and stubble, snails, and various insects. Adults, both male and female, have chestnut-colored breasts, black bellies, and fancy red-pink bills that contrast with their silvery-colored faces. Light pink legs and feet add to their charm. These birds fly with long necks extended and legs trailing, and their wings flash a bold black-and-white pattern. They are vocal in flight, uttering a repeated whistling *pe-che-che*. Formerly called black-bellied tree ducks because of a propensity for perching in trees, they often nest in natural cavities in ebony, live oak, cottonwood, or willow, and may also utilize nesting boxes. They are uncommon and localized in the Southwest and are found primarily along the Mexican border but range as far south as northern Argentina.

Scaled Quail

Callipepla squamata

SPANISH: *Codorniz escamosa, Codorniz crestiblanca*

FAMILY: New World Quail–Odontophoridae

LENGTH & WINGSPAN: 10 inches; 14 inches

Widespread in dry Southwestern grasslands, scaled quail is a pale gray, chicken-like bird with scaly markings on the breast and back. It has a bushy white crest and is frequently called by its nickname: "cotton top." Scaled quail spends most of its time on the ground, tending to run and hide in dense cover rather than fly if pursued. In the spring, males call from the top of fence posts or exposed rocks to attract females and establish breeding territories. The nest site is a hollow depression on the ground, lined with grass and usually well hidden under a shrub, tumbleweed, cactus, or other cover. Young birds depart from the nest shortly after hatching and begin feeding themselves. Main foods include seeds, grains, grass blades, grasshoppers, and other insects.

Gambel's Quail

Callipepla gambelii

SPANISH: *Codorniz de Gambel, Codorniz desértica*

FAMILY: New World Quail–Odontophoridae

LENGTH & WINGSPAN: 10 inches; 14 inches

Gambel's quail are plump, ground-dwelling birds with plumed topknots. They were named after William Gambel, a naturalist from the Academy of Natural Sciences of Philadelphia, who reported seeing these birds while collecting plants and animals along the Santa Fe Trail in 1841. During the winter, Gambel's quail form large groups, or coveys. Members of the covey maintain contact with one another through a series of clucking, crowing calls and are sometimes quite loud and boisterous. In spring, males perch high in shrubs or trees and give clear descending calls to attract mates. For their nests, they use shallow depressions lined with grass, leaves, and twigs, and females often will lay up to a dozen eggs. The downy young leave the nest within a day of hatching and begin life by following their parents around. The attrition rate among young birds is quite high; a mated pair will be fortunate to end up with three or four young from the original brood. To roost safely at night, Gambel's quail retreat into trees and often sleep within the protection of desert mistletoe clumps.

Female (left) and male (right) Gambel's quail

Female (shown on right) with young

Montezuma Quail

Cyrtonyx montezumae
SPANISH: *Codorniz Moctezuma*
FAMILY: New World Quail–Odontophoridae
LENGTH & WINGSPAN: 8¾ inches; 15 inches

Male

When confronted with danger these reticent, difficult-to-see birds freeze on the ground, taking wing only if pressed. The genus name *Cyrtonyx* comes from the Greek *kyrtos*, meaning "curved" or "arched," and *onyx*, meaning "nail" or "claw"—a reference to their long curved claws, an adaptation that enables them to dig in the ground for grass bulbs. Other sources of food include seeds, acorns, juniper berries, caterpillars, and beetles. Named in honor of the last Aztec emperor of Mexico at the time of the Spanish conquest, Montezuma quail reach their northerly limits in areas of Texas, New Mexico, and Arizona, where they inhabit oak canyons and wooded mountain slopes scattered with bunchgrasses. Males have puffy-looking heads brazenly patterned in black, white, and brown. A formerly used common name was harlequin quail, while some call them "crazy" or "fool quail" because of their clownish appearance.

Female

Great Blue Heron

Ardea herodias

SPANISH: *Garzón cenizo, Garza morena,*
Garza blanca grande

FAMILY: Bitterns and Herons–Ardeidae

LENGTH & WINGSPAN: 46 inches; 72 inches

Majestic and grand in stature, the great blue heron is the largest member of its family in North America. In flight, it folds its neck into an S-shape, extends its legs, and flies with deep, slow wingbeats. Great blue herons hunt by slowly wading in shallow water or walking on the ground. Spotting a likely fish or frog, they rapidly thrust their heads forward, catch the prey in their spear-like bills, and swallow it whole. Although they eat mainly fish, they also consume rodents, birds, and reptiles, and are often seen away from water. Great blues are usually silent, except during the nesting season. They nest in colonies high up in trees to discourage predators. Their large, bulky nests made of sticks and twigs may be as far as three miles away from their main feeding sites. Great blue herons have a special adaptation for night vision, enabling them to hunt in dim light.

White-faced Ibis

Plegadis chihi

SPANISH: *Ibis de cara blanca*

FAMILY: Ibises and Roseate
Spoonbills–Threskiornithidae

LENGTH & WINGSPAN: 23 inches;
36 inches

White-faced ibises are wading birds with long necks and long legs. At home in wet agricultural fields and around freshwater ponds, they stick their heads into shallow water, probing for delectable items such as crayfish, frogs, snails, earthworms, and insects. The genus name *Plegadis* is Greek for "sickle" or "scythe," in recognition of the distinctive shape of their lengthy, downward-curving bills. In winter white-faced ibises look dark all over, but during breeding season both male and female show chestnut on the head, neck, and undersides, as well as a purplish bronzy green iridescence on the wings and back. The white "face," present in breeding plumage, is actually a narrow band of white feathers surrounding red facial skin. White-faced ibises are sociable birds, traveling and feeding in flocks, as well as nesting in small colonies. In most areas of the Southwest they are migratory, but some individuals live year-round in certain locations in southern California.

Black Vulture

Coragyps atratus
SPANISH: *Zopilote común*
FAMILY: New World Vultures–Cathartidae
LENGTH & WINGSPAN: 25 inches; 59 inches

The species name *atratus* means "cloaked in black," an appropriate name for this sinister-looking bird with its wrinkly, unfeathered head. Like their turkey vulture cousins, these birds carry out nature's janitorial services by eating the carcasses of dead animals. Sexes are similar, overall black in color with short square tails and whitish patches near the tips of the wings. The male courts the female by ambulating about on the ground, strutting with his wings partly spread, and bobbing his furrowed gray head, sometimes hissing in the process. The female generally lays two eggs on bare ground, in a hollowed-out log or stump, or beneath a large boulder. On occasion, nest sites are decorated with shiny objects such as bits of broken glass or old bottle caps. When faced with extreme heat, black vultures may wet their legs with their own urine as a means of

cooling off. Black vultures are resident in the southeastern U.S., from central Texas northeast to Pennsylvania and New York, but in the West are found only in south-central Arizona, where they are uncommon and localized.

Turkey Vulture

Cathartes aura

SPANISH: *Zopilote aura, Aura cabecirroja, Aura común*

FAMILY: New World Vultures–Cathartidae

LENGTH & WINGSPAN: 26 inches; 67 inches

These strange-looking birds with naked red heads are nearly eagle sized, and their scientific name *Cath-artes* means "purifier." Turkey vultures are purifiers in the sense that they feed primarily on dead animals, serving as nature's clean-up crew. They have a highly developed sense of sight. Also, unlike most birds, they have a keen sense of smell, which enables them to locate carcasses from great distances. When not breeding, turkey vultures use communal roosts at night, ranging in size from a few birds to several hundred. At dusk, spectacular flights may be seen as great numbers glide in to the roost. In the morning, they often hold their wings spread to the sun before flying off for the day. Their flight pattern is rather tilted or teetering, and typically the wings are set in a shallow "V" shape. Turkey vultures have no real voice; they make hissing and puffing sounds at times. They are common summer residents in open country in much of the Southwest.

Cooper's Hawk

Accipiter cooperii

SPANISH: *Gavilán de Cooper, Ésmerejón de Cooper, Gavilán pechirrufo mayor, Gavilán palomero*

FAMILY: Hawks, Kites, and Eagles–Accipitridae

LENGTH & WINGSPAN: 16½ inches; 31 inches

Cooper's hawks are part of a group called "accipiters." The family name Accipitridae comes from *accipere,* meaning "to seize," a reference to the hunting habits of this family of birds. Cooper's hawks have long tails and rounded wings, characteristics that enable the birds to deftly maneuver in dense vegetation. They may be found in river groves and open woodlands as well as in cities and towns. Sometimes called "bird hawks" because of their preference for eating smaller birds, they will also take small-sized mammals. Cooper's hawks and other accipiters are thought to be among nature's checks on populations of small birds, keeping them from becoming too numerous. During breeding season, after some rather vocal mating rituals, the male and female build a large platform of sticks for their nest, usually in a good-sized tree where it is partially hidden in the shade of the canopy. Females are larger than the males, requiring greater body mass for producing eggs that are quite large in relation to the birds' body size. Cooper's hawks have a distinctive pattern in flight: rapid wingbeats alternating with brief glides.

Harris's Hawk

Parabuteo unicinctus
SPANISH: *Aguililla de Harris, Peuco castellano, Aguililla rojinegra, Aguililla cinchada*
FAMILY: Hawks, Kites, and Eagles–Accipitridae
LENGTH & WINGSPAN: 20 inches; 42 inches

Adult Harris's hawk with nestling

Social by nature, Harris's hawks nest together and hunt cooperatively. Hunting strategies vary. Members of a group may converge on prey from different directions, making escape difficult. One or two individuals may pursue the prey into cover while the other birds in the group watch and then attack when the mammal or bird is flushed out. Harris's hawks are very adept at maneuvering and are capable of lightning-fast acceleration. Captured food is shared among members of the social unit, though the dominant birds of the group eat first. These handsome hawks are a rich chocolate brown with chestnut-colored markings on the wings and leg feathers. Their tails have a white base and are tipped with a white band. They sometimes build their nests cradled in the arms of a saguaro cactus. Scattered populations of Harris's hawks may be found in Arizona, New Mexico, and Texas.

Gray Hawk
Buteo nitidus
SPANISH: *Aguililla gris*
FAMILY: Hawks, Kites, and
Eagles–Accipitridae
LENGTH & WINGSPAN: 17 inches;
34 inches

Gray hawks reside along the U.S. border with Mexico during the spring and summer breeding season. Their usual haunts are stands of cottonwoods and willows adjacent to streams. These are handsome hawks, compact in size with gray backs and finely barred underparts alternating in white and gray. As they soar through the air, broad black-and-white tail bands are visible. Swift in flight, gray hawks plummet to the ground in order to capture lizards or snakes, their dietary preferences. They may also feast on small mammals such as rabbits and mice, fish, young birds, and beetles. During courtship both sexes circle in the air, calling out with distinctive, mournful-sounding cries that carry far. For their nest they make a flimsy, shallow platform of sticks lined with green-leaved twigs, generally some seventy feet above ground on the branch of a cottonwood tree. The species name *nitidus* means "bright and shining" in Latin.

Zone-tailed Hawk

Buteo albonotatus
SPANISH: *Aguililla aura*
FAMILY: Hawks, Kites, and
Eagles–Accipitridae
LENGTH & WINGSPAN: 20
inches; 51 inches

Zone-tailed hawks are often overlooked—dismissed as turkey vultures because of their similar appearance in flight. Both have two-toned underwings and fly with wings uptilted in a dihedral or V-shaped pattern. Although this sooty black hawk may look like a turkey vulture at a distance, closer inspection reveals a feathered head, moderately long tail with two narrow white bands, and a yellow cere and feet. (The "cere" is a dense fleshy membrane saddled at the base of the upper mandible surrounding the nostrils in certain species of birds, including raptors.) The zone-tailed's mimicry of the turkey vulture serves it well. Small animals have learned that vultures do not pose any sort of threat and, with guards let down, may be tricked by the sudden appearance of the marauding hawk. Lizards, small mammals, and birds are favored foods of this raptor. Zone-taileds are chiefly spring and summer residents in the Southwest, but some individuals may winter over in the lowlands.

Red-tailed Hawk

Buteo jamaicensis
SPANISH: *Aguililla cola roja, Aguililla parda, Aguililla colirrufa*
FAMILY: Hawks, Kites, and Eagles–Accipitridae
LENGTH & WINGSPAN: 19 inches; 49 inches

This common and widespread bird of prey has a stout body and broad wings and is often seen perching on telephone or roadside poles. When it sees a tasty rabbit, the redtail (as they are commonly called) will glide downward, thrust its legs forward, and make impact with one foot slightly in front of the other. With slow, ponderous wing-beats, and with the prey dangling in its feet, the hawk flies to a perch to feed. During courtship, males and females perform impressive aerial maneuvers, and their acrobatics are often accompanied by sharp, shrill cries. Males frequently catch food and pass it to the female while in the air. Red-tailed hawks live in a wide range of elevations and habitats. Adults almost always have reddish upper tails, but body plumage can vary from pale to dark brown.

Golden Eagle

Aquila chrysaetos
SPANISH: *Águila real*
FAMILY: Hawks, Kites, and Eagles–Accipitridae
LENGTH & WINGSPAN: 30 inches; 79 inches

The golden eagle is one of our most magnificent birds of prey. It is important to many Native American tribes, who admire the bird for its strength and courage. Eagles are widespread in open terrain, where they may soar effortlessly for hours, looking for small mammals such as ground squirrels, jackrabbits, and voles. They've been known to take larger prey such as foxes and cranes, and even young deer. Mostly dark brown in color, golden eagles have a golden wash on the back of the neck; hence the name. Nests are most often on a cliff ledge, where the birds build a bulky platform of sticks, and they often use the same site year after year. New materials are added each year, sometimes doubling the size of the nest. These birds have a high percentage of nesting failure, thought to be due to human disturbance near nests, which causes adults to abandon the eggs.

American Kestrel

Falco sparverius
SPANISH: *Cernícalo americano,*
Halcón cernícalo
FAMILY: Caracaras and Falcons–
Falconidae
LENGTH & WINGSPAN: 9 inches;
22 inches

Also known as sparrow hawk, this bird is actually a member of the falcon family. Kestrels are common and widespread and are found in many different habitats, from open country to cities. The handsome males have blue-gray wings and reddish-brown backs and tails. Both male and female have black-and-white face patterns with dark mustache marks. Grasshoppers are among their favored foods, but they also eat beetles, moths, caterpillars, voles, mice, and small birds. They hunt mainly by watching from a high perch, often from power poles or lines, then swooping down to capture prey with their feet. Kestrels also may hover low in the air over fields, rapidly beating their wings as they anticipate the appearance of a large insect or a small rodent. These small falcons have a habit of moving their tails up and down several times, particularly after alighting on a pole or tree. They nest in tree cavities, and often in old woodpecker holes in saguaro cacti. Kestrels often are attracted to grass fires, where they hunt along the edges for creatures that have been displaced by the flames.

Peregrine Falcon

Falco peregrinus
SPANISH: *Halcón peregrino*
FAMILY: Caracaras and Falcons–Falconidae
LENGTH & WINGSPAN: 16 inches; 41 inches

Peregrine falcons are found on six continents, but they tend to be uncommon everywhere. Among the world's fastest and most agile birds, they may reach speeds of up two hundred miles per hour as they dive from great heights to strike at prey. Adults have slate-gray backs and light-colored chests, and are barred and spotted below. Their strong facial markings are distinctive: they have dark sideburns, or mustache

marks, which are very visible, even in flight. Formerly known as duck hawks, peregrines often are found near water and have a preference for feeding on ducks and shorebirds. They are found in a number of other habitats as well. In cities, some individuals nest on building ledges, where they feed on pigeons. In natural habitat, they nest on cliff ledges and often use the same site for many years. In the mid-twentieth century there was a widespread failure of these birds to reproduce. Studies indicated that this was due to the thinning of their eggshells, a direct effect of the use of DDT and other pesticides. With the subsequent ban on the use of DDT, their numbers have rebounded.

American Coot
Fulica americana
SPANISH: *Gallareta americana*
FAMILY: Rails and Gallinules–Rallidae
LENGTH & WINGSPAN: 15½ inches; 24 inches

These water-birds are at home on the golf course

and at ponds in city parks. Gregarious by nature, they are usually in flocks and can be quite noisy and aggressive. Coots are related to rails but swim like ducks, and they may be seen walking about on shorelines and grass. They have strong, yellowish-green legs and big feet with lobed toes. As they swim through the water, they have a habit of pumping their small heads back and forth. When taking flight from water, they run across the surface and flap their wings furiously before they are able to become airborne. Coots eat mostly plant material, including algae, sedges, and grasses, but also consume insects, tadpoles, fish, snails, and crayfish.

Sandhill Crane

Grus canadensis
SPANISH: *Grulla gris, Grulla cenicienta, Grulla del Canada*
FAMILY: Cranes–Gruidae
LENGTH & WINGSPAN: 42 inches; 74 inches

Cranes are stately, long-necked, and long-legged birds that feed on land or in shallow water. They are omnivores, consuming a variety of foods, including grain, insects, roots of aquatic plants, rodents, snails, frogs, lizards, and snakes. During migration and over the winter months, sandhill cranes form immense flocks that sometimes seem

to cover the sky. They have a distinctive bugling call that may be heard more than a mile away. Cranes frequently are seen feeding on waste grain in cultivated fields during the day. As evening approaches, they return to roosting sites in shallow water. The dawn flight of large flocks of sandhill cranes is one of the most dramatic of wildlife spectacles. The population that winters in the Southwest migrates north to nest around marshes from the northern contiguous U.S. states to Alaska, and even as far away as Siberia. On their nesting grounds, pairs perform elaborate courtship displays, dancing with spread wings and leaping into the air while calling.

Killdeer
Charadrius vociferus
SPANISH: *Chorlito tildío*
FAMILY: Lapwings and Plovers–Charadriidae
LENGTH & WINGSPAN: 10½ inches; 24 inches

Killdeers are members of the plover family: wading birds with thick necks, short pigeon-like bills, and large, staring eyes. They are widespread and abundant and may be found in fields, airports, lawns, schoolyards, and mudflats. As they fly, killdeers call their names with a noisy and insistent *kill-deeah*. Males and females look similar, and both have two black bands across the breast. When they fly, white wing stripes and a golden tawny rump are visible. Killdeers nest on the ground, in shallow scrapes in bare soil, or sometimes on lawns or gravel roofs. They are famous for their broken-wing acts, in which they flutter along the ground with one wing out in a show of injury, thereby luring intruders away from their nests.

White-winged Dove

Zenaida asiatica

SPANISH: *Paloma de ala blanca, Paloma aliblanca*

FAMILY: Pigeons and Doves– Columbidae

LENGTH & WINGSPAN: 12 inches; 19 inches

Aptly named for their large white wing-patches, white-winged doves are otherwise mostly grayish brown except for broad white corners on the tail and blue skin surrounding their ruby-red eyes. They are summer visitors to the Southwest and are found in cities and desert, as well as riparian areas. In some desert areas they visit large flowers, apparently for nectar, and are recognized as important pollinators of the giant saguaro cactus. Otherwise, they feed mostly on the ground, seeking seeds, fruits, and berries. Although some individuals remain north of the Mexican border for the winter, most move south in September. They have a harsh cooing call that sounds like *who cooks for you.* Members of the dove and pigeon family are among the few birds that can drink by suction, sticking their bills in water and drinking continuously. Most other birds must take a bill-full of water at a time and then tilt their heads backward to swallow.

Mourning Dove

Zenaida macroura

SPANISH: *Paloma huilota, Huilota*

FAMILY: Pigeons and Doves–Columbidae

LENGTH & WINGSPAN: 12 inches; 18 inches

Mourning doves are less bulky-looking than white-winged doves, and they occur widely throughout North America. Named for their mournful call, these small-headed doves are gray-brown with pointed tails tipped with white. They are a familiar sight around cities and readily nest in trees and shrubs in suburban yards. Courting males approach females by hopping forward stiffly with their chests puffed out, bowing and giving earnest cooing sounds. Prolific nesters, mourning doves may bring off four to six broods per season in some parts of the Southwest. They may

use the same flimsy platform of sticks repeatedly, and the nests look like they could barely hold eggs, let alone young birds. During nesting season, doves produce a milky fluid that is secreted from the wall of the bird's crop, an enlarged pocket of the upper esophagus. Known as pigeon milk, this fluid is rich in fat and protein, and for the first few days after hatching, young birds are fed pure diets of it.

Inca Dove

Columbina inca

SPANISH: *Tórtola de cola larga, Coquita común, Tórtolita*

FAMILY: Pigeons and Doves–Columbidae

LENGTH & WINGSPAN: 8¼ inches; 11 inches

These small gray doves have a scaly appearance and are often found on lawns in Southwestern cities. They act fairly tame and can be approached closely. When they take off, they flash bright chestnut in the wings and white edges to the tail, and their wings make a rattling noise. Inca doves are primarily urban residents and are rarely seen away from civilization. Their two-syllable, monotonous call sounds like *no hope, no hope.* Sensitive to the cold, they sometimes roost together as a group. Several birds may huddle close together, and even on top of one another, as a means of conserving heat. They eat grains, weed and grass seeds, foraging almost entirely on the ground. Like many members of this family, Inca doves regularly swallow small pieces of gravel to aid in the digestion of hard seeds.

Greater Roadrunner

Geococcyx californianus
SPANISH: *Correcaminos norteño, Paisano, Churea*
FAMILY: Cuckoos and Roadrunners–Cuculidae
LENGTH & WINGSPAN: 23 inches; 22 inches

Roadrunners are conspicuous, ground-dwelling cuckoos of open arid country. With their long tails, shaggy crests, and streaky brown appearance, they are unmistakable. They typically walk or run on the ground, occasionally pausing to elevate their tails and to raise and lower the feathers on their heads. Roadrunners have powerful legs that enable them to attain running speeds of more than fifteen miles per hour. They are reluctant fliers, but occasionally fly short distances in response to danger. Roadrunners feed on a variety of snakes, lizards, spiders, scorpions, birds, eggs, rodents, bats, and insects. Larger prey are grasped in their ponderous bills and then killed as the bird ruthlessly strikes the prey against a rock, stick, or the ground. These birds often sunbathe by raising the feathers on their backs to expose black skin, which absorbs solar radiation. Greater roadrunner is the state bird of New Mexico and has been a featured subject of cartoons and folklore.

Western Screech-Owl

Megascops kennicottii
SPANISH: *Tecolote occidental*
FAMILY: Typical Owls–Strigidae
LENGTH & WINGSPAN: 8½ inches; 20 inches

These small owls are common, though often overlooked. They live in a variety of habitats including the Arizona desert, suburban areas, wooded canyons, and riparian zones. Western screech-owls can locate prey by either sound or sight. This bird hunts mainly at dusk and during the night, watching and listening for signs of movement below its perch. When a small mammal or large insect is detected, the western screech-owl swoops down silently to capture the prey. They also are known to catch flying insects in midair. Usually they nest in holes in trees or poles, and often in saguaro cacti. During courtship, males perform a bowing motion, click their bills, and bring food to

Western screech-owl juvenile

the female. Mated pairs may nibble at each other's feathers and call in duet. The western screech-owl's voice is a series of one-pitched tremulous whistles.

Great Horned Owl

Bubo virginianus

SPANISH: *Búho cornudo grande, Búho cornudo americano, Tecolote cornudo*

FAMILY: Typical Owls–Strigidae

LENGTH & WINGSPAN: 22 inches; 44 inches

Great horned owls are massive, powerful birds that are found throughout the Americas. They are extremely adaptable and are equally at home in desert, grassland, and suburban and forest habitats. Great horned owls have excellent vision and hearing. Their eyes don't move, but flexibility in their necks enables them to swivel their heads more

than 180 degrees to look in any direction. They also have large facial-disk feathers that direct sound waves to their ears. They hunt mainly at night, sitting upright on a high perch to wait, watch, and listen for prey. They silently sail down to capture unsuspecting birds or mammals, which they favor. They also take snakes, frogs, smaller owls, hawks,

and scorpions, and have even been known to attack porcupines, often with fatal results—for the owl. Great horned owls do not build their own nests. Instead, they usually use old nests of other large birds such as hawks, eagles, or herons. These owls have distinctive ear tufts, or 'horns,' white bibs, and large, yellow eyes. Their call is a monotonous, deep-toned hoot.

Ferruginous Pygmy-Owl
Glaucidium brasilianum
SPANISH: *Tecolotito común,*
Tecolotito bajeño
FAMILY: Typical Owls–Strigidae
LENGTH & WINGSPAN: 6¾ inches;
12 inches

These small owls are found in desert habitat along the U.S.–Mexico border. Ferruginous pygmy-owls are common and widespread in the American tropics, but are uncommon to rare in their limited U.S. range—south Texas and Arizona. In the Southwest, there has been much concern about the destruction of their habitat due to development. These birds prefer mesquite thickets, desert riparian areas, and saguaro cacti. Like hawks, owls use their feet and talons in defense rather than their bills. This species hunts by day but is most active near dawn and dusk, and feeds on small birds in addition to insects, rodents, and lizards. Notably bold and aggressive for its small size, ferruginous pygmy-owl often is mobbed by smaller birds that recognize its whistled call. It usually nests in holes in trees or in saguaro cacti.

Elf Owl

Microthene whitneyi
SPANISH: *Tecolote enano, Tecolotito colicorto*
FAMILY: Typical Owls–Strigidae
LENGTH & WINGSPAN: 5¾ inches; 13 inches

Elf owls are the smallest owls in the world, only five to six inches tall, and are generally associated with saguaro cacti and desert vegetation in the Southwest. Strictly

nocturnal, they eat mostly insects but occasionally consume small reptiles and mammals. Elf owls sometimes walk on or hang from flowers or foliage, probing for insects attracted to the blooms. Moths, beetles, and crickets make up most of their diet. These tiny, nocturnal birds of prey are known to store some large food items in their nests for later consumption. Male birds show females several nesting cavities, and the pair bond is established when the female accepts food and the nest cavity from the male. Nest sites include old woodpecker holes in trees, columnar cacti, agave and yucca flower stalks, fence posts, and utility poles. Elf owls vocalize mainly at dusk and just before sunrise. They breed in the U.S.–Mexico border region and winter in southern Mexico. Numbers have dwindled along the lower Colorado River and in south Texas, probably due to loss of habitat, but these owls still seem to be abundant in many areas of southern Arizona.

Lesser Nighthawk
Chordeiles acutipennis
SPANISH: *Chotacabras menor, Tapacamino garapena*
FAMILY: Nightjars–Caprimulgidae
LENGTH & WINGSPAN: 9 inches; 22 inches

Lesser nighthawks are desert dwellers of the American Southwest and Central and South America. They are cryptically colored with brown, buff, and black, and have pale, crescent-shaped markings on their throats and on their pointed wings. During the day, they rest quietly on the ground or on a horizontal branch, blending in perfectly with their surroundings. In the evening and early morning they can be seen flying about, often covering considerable distances, searching for airborne insects.

They have large, gaping mouths adapted for sweeping insects out of the air. In cities at night, they are attracted to large light sources, such as those that illuminate parking lots and shopping centers, where insects congregate. They tend to fly low and silently, abruptly swerving and changing speed and direction. Nighthawks obtain some water from their prey, but in hot dry areas they meet their water requirement by making repeated passes over water and drinking from the surface. Nighthawks are members of the nightjar family and are not related to true hawks.

Female

Broad-billed Hummingbird

Cynanthus latirostris

SPANISH: *Colibrí de pico ancho*

FAMILY: Hummingbirds–Trochilidae

LENGTH & WINGSPAN: 4 inches; 5¾ inches

Male broad-billeds are flashy gems, in iridescent shades of green and blue, with a touch of white behind the eyes and bluish-black forked tails; they also sport bright red-orange bills with tips dipped in black. The female broad-billed, unlike most other hummingbirds of the female persuasion, is relatively easy to identify. Pale white lines surround dark cheek patches, and the base of the lower bill mandible is reddish orange; she also flaunts the blue-black tail. Both sexes make a series of dry chattering notes when alarmed. These hummingbirds have a rather limited range but are generally abundant where found—in riparian zones in dry canyons of southeastern Arizona and southwest New Mexico. Most spend the colder months in Mexico, but some over-winter north of the border. Numbers of over-wintering birds appear to be on the rise as they increasingly adapt to the attractions of home gardens. The genus name *Cynanthus* is from the Greek *kyanos*, meaning "blue," and *anthos* meaning "bright"—a reference to the shimmering blue throat of the male.

Male

Black-chinned Hummingbird

Archilochus alexandri

SPANISH: *Colibrí garganta morada,*
Colibrí gorjinegro

FAMILY: Hummingbirds–Trochilidae

LENGTH & WINGSPAN: 3¾ inches; 4¾ inches

The Southwest is well known for its great variety of hummingbird species. Black-chinned hummingbird is named for the male, which has a black chin or throat. In certain light the throat shows an iridescent purple border. The color on the male's throat helps him attract a mate. The male also performs a pendulum-like courtship display, flying back and forth in front of the female in wide, U-shaped arcs, making whirring sounds on each dive. Females build deep cup nests made of plant fibers and plant down, held together with spider webs. They then lay one to three eggs, about the size of lima beans. Nests are strong, yet flexible, and stretch out as the young birds grow. Black-chinned hummingbirds arrive in the Southwest in spring to breed, and are widespread in semi-open arid lowlands, riparian woodlands, and suburbs. In the fall, they depart for their wintering grounds in Mexico.

Anna's Hummingbird

Calypte anna

SPANISH: *Colibrí de cabeza roja,*
Colibrí coronirrojo

FAMILY: Hummingbirds–
Trochilidae

LENGTH & WINGSPAN: 4 inches; 5¼ inches

More vocal than most hummingbirds, the male Anna's hummingbird has a rather unmelodic song: a series of repetitive, scratchy notes, often delivered while perched. As he sings, he frequently moves his head back and forth, flashing the brilliant iridescence of his rose-red crown and throat. Females are plainer, but they usually show a small spot of color on the throat. In attempting to attract a female, the male hovers in midair, delivering his buzzy song, then flies very high and plummets down toward the female. At the end of the dive, he makes a loud popping noise. Individual birds are often seen with extensive pollen deposits on their bills, foreheads and chins, reflecting their importance as pollinators. Hummingbirds feed on nectar as well as on small insects. Their long bills and extensible tongues make them uniquely adapted for probing into tubular-shaped flowers. Anna's hummingbirds were formerly just winter visitors to the Southwest from nesting grounds in California, but they have been breeding in Arizona since the 1960s.

Costa's Hummingbird

Calypte costae
SPANISH: *Colibrí de cabeza violeta,*
Colibrí costa, Colibrí coronivioleta
desértico
FAMILY: Hummingbirds–Trochilidae
LENGTH & WINGSPAN: 3½ inches; 4¾
inches

A bird of the desert Southwest, Costa's hummingbird frequents desert washes, sage scrub, and lower parts of dry canyons. In the Arizona and California deserts, numbers peak in about March or April, when most breeding activity occurs. By May or June, most birds leave the desert scrub and migrate to the Pacific coast. Males have iridescent violet crowns and violet throat patches that sweep back to a sharp point and flare out on either side of the neck. As if looks weren't enough, Costa's hummingbirds perform daring aerial courtship displays. The male rises high in the air, often one hundred feet or more, and then plunges downward, making a shrill, continuous whistle. At the bottom of the dive, he pulls up sharply and flies upward again. All of this is to impress the female, who is perched nearby. Costa's hummingbird was named after Louis Marie Panteleon Costa, a French nobleman of the early 1800s who was interested in many aspects of natural history, including birds.

Broad-tailed Hummingbird

Selasphorus platycercus
SPANISH: *Zumbador de cola ancha,*
Colibrí vibrador, Chupaminto cola ancha
FAMILY: Hummingbirds–Trochilidae
LENGTH & WINGSPAN: 4 inches; 5¼
inches

This classic hummingbird of the mountain West frequents high-elevation meadows and forests, where it feeds on red tubular flowers like penstemon and paintbrush. Adult male broad-tails create distinctive, high-pitched trilling sounds with certain wing feathers while flying, which can be heard as they navigate over the lowlands during migration. Males and females have bronze-green backs, and the males sport brilliant, rosy-pink throats. Hummingbirds have the highest metabolic rate of any animal and, in order to conserve energy, they often lapse into a state of torpor at night. Their temperature drops, and their breathing and heart rates slow. In the morning, they slowly recover from this lethargic state and fly out to begin feeding again.

Elegant trogon, back view

Elegant Trogon

Trogon elegans
SPANISH: *Trogón elegante,*
Trogón colicobrizo
FAMILY: Trogons–Trogonidae
LENGTH & WINGSPAN: 12½ inches;
16 inches

In North America, elegant trogon is one of the most sought-after birds, by birdwatchers from all over the world. Trogons arrive in the Chiricahua, Santa Rita, and Huachuca mountains of southeastern Arizona in late April. There, among the streamside oaks, sycamores, and black walnut trees, they sit quietly, peering about for food. They may hover briefly to pluck fruit or insects from the foliage, and then fly back to another branch. The vividly colored male has a black face and throat, iridescent green breast and upperparts, and a geranium-red belly. Formerly called coppery-tailed trogon, its long, square tail shows coppery-colored highlights at close range. Trogons often nest in abandoned woodpecker holes or natural cavities in sycamores and are quite vulnerable to nest disturbance. In the fall, most migrate south to Mexico, but some will spend the winter along a lowland stream in southeastern Arizona.

Elegant trogon, frontal view

Belted Kingfisher

Ceryle alcyon
SPANISH: *Martín pescador norteño,*
Martín pescador migratorio
FAMILY: Kingfishers–Alcedinidae
LENGTH & WINGSPAN: 13 inches; 20 inches

Kingfishers are solitary birds with large heads and dagger-like bills. With their conspicuous ragged crests and slate-blue backs and breast bands, belted kingfishers are unmistakable. Females are more colorful than the males, with rusty-colored belly-bands. Belted kingfishers make a loud, dry, rattling call that is a familiar sound in areas near open water. They hover over or near the water, waiting for just the right moment to plunge in. With eyes closed, they dive, grabbing fish or other aquatic animals in their bills. Belted kingfishers nest in burrows in the ground. The site is usually a bank devoid of vegetation. Both sexes excavate by slashing at the soil with their bills, and use their feet to remove the dirt. They have very short legs, making efficient movement on land a challenge; they must shuffle in and out of their nesting burrows.

Green Kingfisher

Chloroceryle americana

SPANISH: *Martín pescador menor, Martín pescador verde*

FAMILY: Kingfishers–Alcedinidae

LENGTH & WINGSPAN: 8¾ inches; 11 inches

Smallest of the U.S. kingfishers, green kingfishers can be found along a few streams and rivers near the Mexican border. Flying rapidly with quick wingbeats, they move up- and downstream low over the water. When not airborne, they often are overlooked because they tend to perch low in streamside shrubs and trees. Minnows and other small fish make up most of their diet, but green kingfishers also have been known to feed on some aquatic insects. Green above with white collars, they have white underparts with green spots. Males have bright, rusty breast bands. Like other members of the family, green kingfishers are burrowing nesters. The entrance to the burrow is usually well hidden by overhanging plants or roots.

Acorn Woodpecker

Melanerpes formicivorus

SPANISH: *Carpintero arlequín, Carpintero de bellota*

FAMILY: Woodpeckers–Picidae

LENGTH & WINGSPAN: 9 inches; 17½ inches

Acorn woodpeckers are highly sociable birds, usually living year-round in family groups of up to a dozen or more. They are closely associated with oaks and have a unique method of hoarding acorns in storage trees, or granaries. Acorn granaries are usually in large, dead tree limbs, if available, or sometimes in power poles or buildings. An individual tree may have only a few or as many as fifty thousand individually drilled holes. The habit of storing nuts in granaries is unique to this species. Acorns and other kinds of nuts are eaten when insects, their preferred food, are unavailable. If they exhaust their stores, they may abandon territories and wander off in search of food. Acorn woodpeckers have distinctive, clownish face patterns and are very vocal birds. Family groups may contain as many as seven male breeders that compete with one another to mate with one, two, or three egg-laying females. As many as ten male and female non-breeding birds help to raise the young. Acorn woodpeckers often fly out to catch insects in midair. These forays are often nearly vertical, displaying a surprising level of acrobatic skill.

Gila Woodpecker

Melanerpes uropygialis
SPANISH: *Carpintero del desierto, Carpintero pechileonado desértico, Carpintero de Gila*
FAMILY: Woodpeckers–Picidae
LENGTH & WINGSPAN: 9¼ inches; 16 inches

Gila woodpeckers are cheeky, noisy birds that have adapted well to life in Southwestern cities and suburbs. In the desert, they make their nesting cavities in saguaro cacti. Using their stiff tail feathers and clinging four-toed feet, they are able to brace themselves on vertical surfaces in order to excavate nesting holes. Gila woodpeckers

Gila woodpecker

eat insects, fruit, nectar, seeds, small lizards, earthworms, eggs, and almost anything else that presents itself. They may be a bit of a nuisance at hummingbird feeders, where they siphon off large quantities of sugar water. In the very early hours of the morning, these birds sometimes drum on metal objects—such as coolers and drain pipes—as a way of advertising their territories. Gilas have plain brown heads and underparts, and males sport a rounded red cap on the top of their heads. Their backs are barred with black and white, and there is a small patch of yellow under their tails. They fly with an undulating flight pattern, dipping up and down, and often call in the process.

Ladder-backed Woodpecker

Picoides scalaris

SPANISH: *Carpinterillo mexicano*

FAMILY: Woodpeckers–Picidae

LENGTH & WINGSPAN: 7¼ inches; 13 inches

Less conspicuous than other members of their family, these smallish woodpeckers have black-and-white striped faces, and black and white bars on the back that resemble the steps on a ladder. Males have red caps. Often heard before they are seen, ladder-backed woodpeckers make a sharp *"pik"* call note. They are found year-round in arid country. They nest in holes in trees such as mesquite, willow, and oak. In the absence of trees, they may excavate nest cavities in a dying or dead branch of a Joshua tree, in an agave stalk, or sometimes in a saguaro cactus. Ladder-backs feed on many different kinds of insects, including ants. They also eat berries and cactus fruits.

Arizona Woodpecker

Picoides arizonae

SPANISH: *Carpintero de Arizona*

FAMILY: Woodpeckers–Picidae

LENGTH & WINGSPAN: 7½ inches; 14 inches

Most North American woodpeckers are black and white. This species is set apart by its chocolate-brown color with white trimmings. Males and females look similar, with uniformly brown unmarked backs, underparts with barring and spotting, and large white neck patches. Females lack the decorative patch of red found on the nape of the male. The Arizona woodpecker is found only in southeastern Arizona, where it dwells in pine–oak mountain canyons at elevations of 4,000–7,000 feet. Like other woodpeckers, it travels vertically up tree trunks and over and under large limbs, using its sturdy bill to chisel into the wood in quest of insects and larvae. Woodpecker bills and skulls have evolved so that these birds are able to drum on hard wood without sustaining injury. Muscular pads at the back of the lower jaws act as shock absorbers. After tapping on a trunk or branch, the Arizona woodpecker uses its sense of hearing to detect the presence of insects, able to pick up the distinctive sounds made by disturbed wood-boring larvae.

Gilded Flicker

Colaptes chrysoides
SPANISH: *Carpintero de pechera de Arizona, Carpintero desértico*
FAMILY: Woodpeckers–Picidae
LENGTH & WINGSPAN: 11 inches; 18 inches

    Gilded flickers are woodpeckers that live in the lowlands of the Southwest, mainly in desert areas. Like the Gila woodpecker, they have chisel-like bills and are known for excavating nesting holes in saguaro cacti. These are advantageous nesting sites because they provide protection from predators as well as insulation; it may be ten degrees cooler within the cavity. When gilded flickers fly, they flash a bright golden yellow under their wings and tail. Their bold markings include a black, crescent-shaped patch across the chest, and a white rump patch, which is especially conspicuous in flight. Males have red mustache marks on the face. Flickers spend a lot of time on the ground, where they hop around rather clumsily on their short legs, searching for ants and various other insects to eat. They also consume some fruits and berries.

Northern Beardless-Tyrannulet

Camptostoma imberbe

SPANISH: *Mosquero lampiño*

FAMILY: Tyrant Flycatchers–
Tyrannidae

LENGTH & WINGSPAN: 4½ inches;
7 inches

Granted, the common name is lengthy for such a diminutive bird. This unassuming flycatcher is dubbed "beardless" because it lacks rictal bristles at the base of its flat bill, a characteristic of most flycatchers. (Modified feathers that resemble stiff hairs, rictal bristles fulfill a sensory function. As the bird pursues its prey in midair, the insect becomes difficult to see at the last split second. The sensitive bristles help the bird to sense the insect by touch, at which point it snaps its bill closed with unerring accuracy.) Northern beardless-tyrannulets manage to capture small, slow-moving insects, and eat some seeds and berries as well. These birds are heard more often than seen, which is probably just as well since they are nondescript-looking at best: olive-gray with bushy crests, pale eyebrows, and two drab wing bars. The male's song is a pleasing series of three to five descending whistles: *pee dee dee dee.* These uncommon little flycatchers are summer residents in southern Arizona, southwest New Mexico, and south Texas, frequenting dense streamside stands of mesquite, cottonwood, sycamores, and oaks.

Greater Pewee

Contopus pertinax

SPANISH: *Pibí mayor*

FAMILY: Tyrant Flycatchers–
Tyrannidae

LENGTH & WINGSPAN: 8
inches; 13 inches

This flycatcher is a summer resident in mountain forests of central and southeast Arizona and southwest New Mexico. It is particularly fond of lofty

trees, where it perches to proclaim *ho-say mah-re-ah*, a call that gives it the Spanish nickname of "José María." Chunky and plain-looking, the greater pewee has a pointed crest, a long notched tail, grayish wing bars, and an orange lower mandible to the bill. These birds are known for their great watchfulness around nest sites, patrolling and fending off intruding snakes, squirrels, jays, and hawks. Some believe that other songbirds build their nests in close proximity to the greater pewee in order to take advantage of the protection afforded by this eagle-eyed bird. The pewee assembles a deep cup-shaped nest on a horizontal branch using weed stems, grasses, dry leaves, and lichens; the outside is often bound with spider silk.

Western Wood-Pewee

Contopus sordidulus
SPANISH: *Pibí occidental*
FAMILY: Tyrant Flycatchers–Tyrannidae
LENGTH & WINGSPAN: 6¼ inches; 10½ inches

Western wood-pewees are small, drab-looking flycatchers that are widespread breeders in many areas of the West. They are regarded as habitat generalists because they are able to live in a variety of localities, including ponderosa-pine forests, along mountain streams, and in canyons with sycamores and cottonwoods. They typically perch quietly on high exposed branches, sallying forth to snap up flying insects, and then returning to the same or a nearby perch. They may also hover at leaves or twigs in hopes of gleaning a juicy caterpillar or lacewing. For their nests, they build a flat, open cup composed of grasses and plant parts; the exterior is sometimes adorned with mosses or lichens. Females typically lay three eggs, white in color but decorated with patches of lavender and brown. The species name *sordidulus* is from the Latin *sordidus*, meaning "dirty" or "soiled," a reference to the bird's dullish plumage.

Black Phoebe

Sayornis nigricans
SPANISH: *Papamoscas negro, Mosquero negro*
FAMILY: Tyrant Flycatchers–Tyrannidae
LENGTH & WINGSPAN: 7 inches; 11 inches

This flycatcher, sooty black above and white below, is usually found near water. Proximity to water is necessary because black phoebes use mud to construct their nests. The mud shell is lined with plant materials and is typically located over water and plastered to a vertical wall, often on a bridge or building. Birds characteristically sit on a perch low to the ground, often bobbing their tails, and then suddenly fly out to capture insects in the air, or glean them from the ground or the surface of a pond. They produce a loud, snapping

sound as their bills rapidly close around their prey. They also may hover in the air before swooping to the ground for an insect. The indigestible parts of insects are coughed up later as pellets. The black phoebe's sharp whistled *"fi-bee, fi-bee"* call is a characteristic sound along creeks and ponds in the Southwest.

Say's Phoebe

Sayornis saya

SPANISH: *Papamoscas llanero, Mosquero llanero*

FAMILY: Tyrant Flycatchers–Tyrannidae

LENGTH & WINGSPAN: 7½ inches; 13 inches

Say's phoebes are delicately hued flycatchers of open country. Mostly gray-brown with blackish tails, they have pale, cinnamon-colored bellies. Their call note is a soft whistled *pee-ee*. Like other flycatchers, Say's phoebes are insect eaters, consuming wild bees and wasps as well as flies, beetles, and grasshoppers. They typically perch within a few feet of the ground, making direct flights out into the air to capture prey. Say's phoebes frequently build their nests on a rocky ledge or under the supporting shelf of an abandoned building, and often reuse old nests. Human-made structures, which provide suitable nesting sites, have undoubtedly benefited this species. They are year-round residents in the Southwest.

Vermilion Flycatcher

Pyrocephalus rubinus

SPANISH: *Mosquero cardenalito*

FAMILY: Tyrant Flycatchers–Tyrannidae

LENGTH & WINGSPAN: 6 inches; 10 inches

Males of this species are a flaming scarlet color. Actually the upperparts and tail are brown, and brown extends through the eye, producing a masked appearance. But it is the radiant red of these birds that catches the eye. Females are more subtle-looking, with narrow streaks on light-colored breasts and bellies washed with a soft salmon color. Male vermilion flycatchers perform a fascinating courtship display. Puffing out their feathers, they ascend fifty feet or more into the air, singing and hovering with rapidly beating wings. Then with a slow fluttering flight, they descend and swoop back to their favorite perch. These birds are particularly fond of the edges of streams and ponds, and feed mainly on flying insects. They can be found from the southwestern U.S. to Argentina.

Dusky-capped Flycatcher

Myiarchus tuberculifer

SPANISH: *Copetón triste*

FAMILY: Tyrant Flycatchers–Tyrannidae

LENGTH & WINGSPAN: 7¼ inches; 10 inches

The dusky-capped flycatcher is the smallest member of the *Myiarchus* genus in the Southwest. The name comes from the Greek *myia*, meaning "fly," and *archos*, which

means "ruler." This bird is often difficult to see, but has a distinctive cry that aids in its identification—a melancholy, downward-slurring whistle. A summer resident, it arrives in April and takes up residence along streams and waterways lined with cottonwoods and sycamores, or in mountain canyons with pines and oaks, generally below 6,000 feet. For its nest, the dusky-capped flycatcher utilizes abandoned woodpecker holes or natural hollows in trees or stumps, to which it adds various plant parts including twigs, leaves, bark, and grasses. Plant down or animal hair is often used to line and soften the nest. In typical flycatcher fashion, dusky-caps make aerial sorties in order to catch flying insects, but they also hover at the leaves of shrubs and trees to glean leafhoppers, beetles, spittlebugs, bees, and wasps.

Ash-throated Flycatcher

Myiarchus cinerascens

SPANISH: *Copetón cenizo, Papamoscas copetón gorjicenizo*

FAMILY: Tyrant Flycatchers–Tyrannidae

LENGTH & WINGSPAN: 8½ inches; 12 inches

Ash-throated flycatchers are known for sometimes choosing unusual sites for their nests, such as drainpipes or empty mailboxes. They also may nest in old woodpecker holes in trees or in saguaro cacti. Both sexes participate in nest building, collecting masses of weeds, grass, and twigs to line the cavity. Grayish-brown above and pale yellow below, they have reddish brown on the wings and tail. Like other members of the flycatcher family, they have bushy heads, giving them a crested appearance, and they feed mainly on insects. They also consume fruits and berries, including those of the saguaro cactus and desert mistletoe. Ash-throated flycatchers are common and widespread in arid country. Most individuals depart from the U.S. in fall, but some spend the winter in southwestern Arizona and southern California.

Brown-crested Flycatcher
Myiarchus tyrannulus
SPANISH: *Copetón tirano*
FAMILY: Tyrant Flycatchers–Tyrannidae
LENGTH & WINGSPAN: 8¾ inches; 13 inches

The species name *tyrannulus* means "little tyrant" or "little monarch," appropriate designations for these feisty flycatchers. When the birds arrive in late spring to breed, they are noticeable: raucous, rowdy, and hawkish in terms of protecting their nesting territories. Their call has been described as a strident *pwit* or rolling *purreet*. While at home in riparian areas with cottonwoods, willows, and sycamores, brown-crested flycatchers also live in desert areas where they often nest in abandoned woodpecker holes in saguaro cacti. These birds are similar in appearance to both the dusky-capped and ash-throated flycatchers, but are the largest of the three. They have thicker bills and bushier crests, giving them a larger-headed appearance. Brown-crested flycatchers consume beetles and any number of flying insects as well as wild berries. They are also known for snagging small hummingbirds for a tasty repast.

Sulphur-bellied Flycatcher
Myiodynastes luteiventris
SPANISH: *Papamoscas atigrado, Papamoscas rayado cejiblanco, Papamoscas vientre-amarillo*
FAMILY: Tyrant Flycatchers–Tyrannidae
LENGTH & WINGSPAN: 8½ inches; 14½ inches

Primarily a species of the tropics, sulphur-bellied flycatchers migrate northward to a few areas in southeastern Arizona for the breeding season. They usually nest in the natural cavities of large sycamores in streamside canyons near the Mexican border. During the nesting season, they are very aggressive and often compete for choice nesting spots with other hole-nesting birds, including larger ones such as elegant trogon. Sulphur-bellied flycatchers are colorful and strongly patterned. They have bright, reddish-brown tails, a black mask through the eye, and conspicuous, dark streaks on their sulphur-yellow underparts. Courtship between male and female involves perching close together with both individuals shaking their heads back and forth and calling in duet. Their shrill call sounds like a squeaky rubber toy. These streaked flycatchers leave the Southwest in September, flying to South America to spend the winter.

Cassin's Kingbird

Tyrannus vociferans
SPANISH: *Tirano gritón*
FAMILY: Tyrant Flycatchers–Tyrannidae
LENGTH & WINGSPAN: 9 inches; 16 inches

Kingbirds are medium-sized flycatchers known for their aggressive behavior, and Cassin's kingbird is often seen harassing larger birds, such as ravens or hawks, that dare to venture near its nest. Usually built in trees such as sycamores, cottonwoods, oaks, or

pines, the nests are large, bulky structures. During courtship, male birds may display by flying in a fast, zigzag pattern. Members of a pair often perch together in the nest tree, with their wings quivering and calling loudly. The scientific name *vociferans*—from the Latin "to cry out or be clamorous"—is appropriate for Cassin's kingbird because often it is noisier than other kingbirds. This species captures flying insects in midair but also may hover at leaves to pick them off. They also eat some berries and fruit, more than most flycatchers.

Western Kingbird
Tyrannus verticalis
SPANISH: *Tirano de bordes blancos,*
Madrugador avispero, Tirano palido
FAMILY: Tyrant Flycatchers–Tyrannidae
LENGTH & WINGSPAN: 8¾ inches;
15½ inches

Perching western kingbirds are a typical sight along roadside fences in open country. These spunky, adaptable birds breed in the western U.S. and winter in southeastern Mexico and Central America. The males perform frenzied courtship displays, ascending some fifty feet into the air and then tumbling downwards, all the while fluttering and vibrating their feathers. Mated pairs frequently use human-made structures for nesting, often placing their open, cup-shaped nests on the crossbars of telephone poles or sometimes on building ledges or towers. Nests are constructed from various plant parts and lined with soft materials such as hair, feathers, and even scraps of paper. Like their relatives, they vigorously defend their nesting territories, making harsh, buzzing calls as they attack intruders. Males and females look alike, patterned with a pale-gray head and breast, yellow underparts, and black tail with white outer edges.

Rose-throated Becard
Pachyramphus aglaiae
SPANISH: *Mosquero cabezón degollado*
FAMILY: Tyrant Flycatchers–Tyrannidae
LENGTH & WINGSPAN: 7¼ inches; 12 inches

Although considered part of the flycatcher family, this bird is not as closely related as other members of this group. It has a distinctive shape: a thickset neck with short tail and bill. Males are gray above, with dark caps and a rose-colored patch on the throat; hence the name.

Females are buffy brown with dark caps as well. Small numbers of these tropical birds reach the U.S. in Arizona, southwestern New Mexico, and south Texas during the breeding season. They are difficult to see because they often perch motionless for seemingly long periods of time. The becard's nest is a globular affair, with an entrance hole on the side, usually positioned towards the end of a long branch. The female is thought to do the bulk of the nest-building, using bark, grass, leaves, and plant stems. In subsequent years, becards often return to the same nest site, or at least very close to it.

Loggerhead Shrike
Lanius ludovicianus
SPANISH: *Alcaudón verdugo, Alcaudón yanqui, Lanion americano*
FAMILY: Shrikes–Laniidae
LENGTH & WINGSPAN: 9 inches; 12 inches

Boldly patterned birds, loggerhead shrikes are bluish-gray above with black facial masks and black wings and tails. In flight, they show white patches in the wings. A popular name for this bird is "butcherbird" or "thornbird" because of its habit of impaling prey on sharp objects such as thorns or barbed wire. Impaling enables the bird to immobilize larger prey than it could otherwise handle, and is also a means of food storage. Though lacking the strong feet and talons of hawks and eagles, shrikes do have hooked bills, which enable them to tear at the flesh of large prey. These masked hunters occupy a unique position in the food chain because they are both songbirds and top-level predators. They feed on a variety of creatures, including amphibians, small reptiles, mammals, and birds. Shrikes usually are found in open country with short vegetation, and near agricultural fields and golf courses. In recent decades, populations of this species have declined, thought to be due to changes in habitat and the use of pesticides.

Bell's Vireo

Vireo bellii

SPANISH: *Vireo de Bell*

FAMILY: Vireos–Vireonidae

LENGTH & WINGSPAN: 4¾ inches; 7 inches

Vireos are small song-birds closely related to wood-warblers. Generally dressed in drab shades of olive green, vireos often show some sort of pattern around the eye. They feed primarily on insects and their larvae, which they methodically glean from the leaves of trees and shrubs, but berries are also part of the diet at certain seasons. Bell's vireo was named by John James Audubon for John Graham Bell, a taxidermist who accompanied Audubon on his 1843 Missouri River Expedition. During spring and summer, Bell's vireos take up residence in riparian areas with willows and mesquites in the western U.S. and northern Mexico. Their scrambling, yet musical, songs sound as if the birds are answering themselves. Roger Tory Peterson described it as: *"cheedle cheedle chee?? cheedle cheedle chew."* These melodic embellishments more than make up for the bird's drab appearance: both males and females are gray above with one white wing bar, a faint eyeline, and indistinct "spectacles" around the eyes.

Steller's Jay

Cyanocitta stelleri

SPANISH: *Chara crestada, Chara copetona*

FAMILY: Jays and Crows–Corvidae

LENGTH & WINGSPAN: 11½ inches; 19 inches

This feisty member of the jay family was named after Georg Wilhelm Steller, a German zoologist who first encountered these birds along the coast of Alaska in 1741. Steller's jays are imposing, dark-blue birds with long crests. They are familiar visitors to picnic areas and campgrounds at high elevations. They hop about on the ground or from branch to branch, begging for morsels of cheese, bread, or anything else that is available.

Like other birds in this family, Steller's jays are omnivores and eat a wide variety of plant and animal food. Once an individual bird has been fed at the picnic table, other members of the flock suddenly may come swooping in, announcing their arrival with loud, clamorous calls. Steller's jays often imitate the sounds of other animals, including flickers, hawks, and squirrels. They are permanent residents through most of their range, but some high-elevation populations may migrate to lower elevations in the winter in response to food shortages.

Western Scrub-Jay

Aphelocoma californica
SPANISH: *Chara californiana, Chara pechirrayada*
FAMILY: Jays and Crows–Corvidae
LENGTH & WINGSPAN: 11½ inches; 15½ inches

Western scrub-jays are birds of the oak, piñon, and juniper woodlands, and are usually found in raucous, noisy groups. As they fly, they flap their wings vigorously a few times and then spread their wings and tails stiffly, pitching forward. The western scrub-jay has a blue head, blue wings, and a long blue tail. A streaked, blue-gray band that resembles a necklace sets off its light-colored throat. Diet varies with the season and the region in which they live. In summer, they consume many insects, as well as some spiders and snails.

During the winter months, they feed on acorns, pinecone and other seeds, and nuts and berries. They also are known for taking eggs from other birds' nests, as well as young nestlings.

Mexican Jay

Aphelocoma ultramarina

SPANISH: *Chara de pecho gris, Grajo azul, Chara azulosa, Chara pechigrís*

FAMILY: Jays and Crows–Corvidae

LENGTH & WINGSPAN: 11½ inches; 19½ inches

Unlike most jays that breed in isolated pairs, Mexican jays nest in cooperative flocks, and groups of five to twenty-five individuals defend permanent territories. Within each territory, several females may breed simultaneously. Young are fed not only by their parents, but also by other members of the group. Some individuals may live twenty years, often in the company of their own offspring and other relatives on the same territory where they were hatched. Individuals may come and go, but the groups persist over time, and territorial boundaries rarely change. Mexican jays are resident in pine-oak-juniper woodlands, and rely heavily on acorns and piñon nuts to survive the winter. In September and October when the acorns are fresh, they stash nuts in the ground. Grasping an acorn in their bills, they thrust it into the soil or leaf litter. Some individuals apparently have sufficient long-term memory to recall the location of the stored nuts.

Chihuahuan Raven

Corvus cryptoleucus

SPANISH: *Cuervo llanero*

FAMILY: Jays and Crows–Corvidae

LENGTH & WINGSPAN: 19½ inches; 44 inches

Common Raven

Corvus corax

SPANISH: *Cuervo común, Cuervo grande*

FAMILY: Jays and Crows–Corvidae

LENGTH & WINGSPAN: 24 inches; 53 inches

Poets and authors have mythologized these highly intelligent and adaptable members of the crow family as figures of death, danger, and wisdom. They are large birds, mostly or entirely black, and have very heavy bills. They are omnivorous and consume practically anything, regularly feeding on carrion, garbage, insects, rodents, lizards, frogs, and the eggs and young of other birds. Skillful fliers, ravens seem almost playful at times as they wheel and swoop through the air. Their loud, cacophonous calls carry for long distances. Chihuahuan and common ravens differ only slightly in appearance. Chihuahuans, sometimes called white-necked ravens, are slightly smaller and have white bases to the feathers on the neck and breast. The white is seen only when the feathers are blown in a certain way. Chihuahuan ravens tend to live in arid and semi-arid grasslands and scrub, and generally avoid both wooded areas and true deserts. Common ravens live in a broader range of habitats, including drier places such as deserts and wetter areas like mountain forests, but they are seldom seen in grassland. Like other members of this family, they cache or store away a variety of foods in all seasons, to be eaten later.

Horned Lark

Eremophila alpestris
SPANISH: *Alondra cornuda*
FAMILY: Larks–Alaudidae
LENGTH & WINGSPAN: 7¼ inches; 12 inches

The horned lark is the only representative of the lark family that is native to North America. It is a brown, ground-dwelling bird with black sideburns, two small black "horns" on the top of the head, and a black breast mark. The horns are actually occipital feather tufts that can be raised or lowered, and usually are visible only at close range. Groups of horned larks are common in sparsely vegetated open country. They eat mainly weed and grass seeds, and often feed on waste grains in livestock feedlots or on crop stubble in agricultural areas. They frequently sing in flight. Most larks live in open country, where there are no high perches from which to sing. Perhaps as a result, many species have developed flight-song displays to advertise their claims to the nesting territory on the ground below.

Purple Martin

Progne subis
SPANISH: *Golondrina azul-negra*
FAMILY: Swallows–Hirundinidae
LENGTH & WINGSPAN: 8 inches; 15½–16 ¾ inches

Swallows are agile, graceful fliers that feed primarily on the wing. The largest member of this group in North America is the purple martin, a slender bird with long pointed wings and a forked tail. As it flies through the air with mouth agape, it

Male

Female purple martin

takes in armies of flying insects. Males are a glossy purplish-black all over; females are dark above and gray below, with whitish foreheads and collars. Purple martins are cavity-nesters, and in the West they use abandoned woodpecker holes, crevices in cliffs, or human-made objects such as drainpipes. In desert regions they utilize cavities in saguaro cacti. These skillful aerialists drink and bathe on the wing. In late summer, before returning to their South American wintering range, they often roost together in large groups—sometimes by the thousands. The genus name *Progne* is Greek after Procne, daughter of Pandion, King of Athens, who was turned into a swallow after committing a dastardly deed.

Cliff Swallow

Petrochelidon pyrrhonota
SPANISH: *Golondrina risquera, Golondrina castaña*
FAMILY: Swallows–Hirundinidae
LENGTH & WINGSPAN: 5½ inches; 13½ inches

Cliff swallows live in a variety of habitats, including grasslands, canyons, riparian areas, and cities. They are long-distance migrants, wintering in South America. Each spring, the birds return to North America in

search of nesting sites, which often include highway culverts, bridges, and buildings. They are very sociable birds and tend to nest in large colonies. Proximity to mud from stream banks, lakes, or temporary puddles is necessary for breeding. Both sexes gather mud in their bills and bring it back to the colony, where it is molded into a gourd-shaped nest. Individual birds sometimes fight aggressively for nests in the center of the colony rather than near the edges, where they would be more vulnerable to predators. Cliff swallows drink by flying low over water, skimming the surface, and lapping up the water. Recognized by their square tails, orange rumps, and chestnut-colored throats, cliff swallows also have triangular forehead patches that may be white, creamy, or chestnut.

Mexican Chickadee
Poecile sclateri
SPANISH: *Carbonero mexicano, Mascarita*
FAMILY: Chickadees and Titmice–Paridae
LENGTH & WINGSPAN: 5 inches; 8¼ inches

There is no other word for the chickadees—they are "cute." Mexican chickadees have a limited range: the high-elevation pine and fir forests of the Chiricahua Mountains in southeastern Arizona and the Animas Mountains in New Mexico, where they are the only chickadees in residence. Males and females are identical in appearance. They sport dark black bibs and caps set against a white cheek, charcoal-colored flanks, and gray wings, each with one narrow light wing bar. These sprightly birds sing cheerful tunes as they make abbreviated flights through the trees in search of caterpillars and insects. The chickadee's name is what we call "onomatopoeic," which means that its common name imitates the sound of the bird: in this case *chick-a-dee-dee-dee*. Mexican chickadees nest in natural cavities in tree trunks or branches, and often use animal hair to provide cozy linings for the five to eight eggs laid by the female.

Bridled Titmouse
Baeolophus wollweberi
SPANISH: *Carbonero embridado, Herrelillo enmascarado, Paro embozalado*
FAMILY: Chickadees and Titmice–Paridae
LENGTH & WINGSPAN: 5¼ inches; 8 inches

These small, perky birds have striking black-and-white face patterns, black bibs, and jaunty crests. The black-and-white markings on the head suggest the outline of a horse's bridle. In the U.S., they are restricted to the mountains of southwestern New

Mexico and central and southern Arizona. Their preferred habitat is oak woodland, but they also may be found in riparian areas and pine–oak woodlands at higher elevations. They chatter frequently as they move about and search for insects in trees. More acrobatic than other titmice, they often hang upside down as they pick insects from the bark or foliage of a tree. During nonbreeding seasons, they sometimes flock with other small birds such as chickadees, kinglets, nuthatches, and creepers. Bridled titmice are cavity nesters.

Verdin

Auriparus flaviceps
SPANISH: *Baloncillo, Párido del desértico*
FAMILY: Verdin–Remizidae
LENGTH & WINGSPAN: 4½ inches; 6½ inches

Verdins are tiny, active birds of hot desert regions and are common around some Southwestern cities. This diminutive little bird is not really as nondescript as one might first think. Though overall a brown-gray color, the adults—both males and females—have yellowish heads. They also have small, chestnut-colored shoulder patches that are often difficult to see. Verdins seem to be on the move almost continuously, flitting nimbly and rapidly about in the vegetation. They often hang upside down as they search for food under branches and leaves. Insects and their larvae, as well as some small fruits and berries, make up most of their diet. However, they also visit flowers, which they grasp with one foot while piercing the bottom to sip the nectar. Like most other birds, verdins build nests in which to raise their young, but they also build nests to sleep in at night. The size of a large softball, nests are roughly spherical in shape with a hollow center and an entrance on the side, and are usually placed in the outer branches of a thorny shrub or low tree, or in cholla cacti.

Cactus Wren

Campylorhynchus brunneicapillus
SPANISH: *Matraca del desierto,*
Matraca grande, Saltapared
FAMILY: Wrens–Troglodytidae
LENGTH & WINGSPAN: 8½ inches;
11 inches

Cactus wrens represent a tropical group of large, sociable wrens. Curious and bold, they have big personalities to match their size. As they move jerkily along, often in small family units, they sometimes flit their wings and tails about expressively, calling to one another all the while. Their voice is a harsh, rasping *"chug, chug, chug, chug,"* which gains in rapidity and sounds something like a car engine trying to start. Both male and female are heavily spotted and streaked in brown, with broad, white lines above red eyes. The top of the head is solid brown. Cactus wrens build massive, bulky nests with an opening at one end. Nesting materials include weeds, grasses, twigs, feathers, hair, and—in areas of human habitation—paper products such as tissue or wax paper. The males may build extra dummy nests while the female is incubating the current brood of young. After the breeding season, they may sleep in these nests at night. Cactus wrens are found in arid country with scrubby brush, cacti, yuccas, and mesquite trees. They eat mostly insects, but also some fruits. Cactus wren is the state bird of Arizona.

Rock Wren

Salpinctes obsoletus

SPANISH: *Saltapared roquero, Troglodita saltarroca*

FAMILY: Wrens–Troglodytidae

LENGTH & WINGSPAN: 6 inches; 9 inches

Rock wrens are pale, gray-brown birds of rocky slopes and canyons in arid country. They have finely streaked breasts, rusty-brown tails, and soft buffy underparts. Rock wrens feed primarily on the ground, using their long bills to probe into rock crevices for insects and spiders. As they move about on the ground, they often pause, bounce up and down several times, and deliver an echoing, metallic call. They build cup nests, usually in the crevice of a boulder or under a rocky ledge. Rock wrens are known for "paving" the ground in front of their nest entrances with small stones, bones, or other debris.

Canyon Wren

Catherpes mexicanus

SPANISH: *Saltapared risquero, Saltapared barranqueño, Troglodita saltapared*

FAMILY: Wrens–Troglodytidae

LENGTH & WINGSPAN: 5¾ inches; 7½ inches

The resonant song of the canyon wren is one of the most beautiful natural sounds of the arid Southwest. It's a melodic outburst of liquid descending notes that echoes through the stream-lined, shady canyons where it lives. With its long, narrow bill and flattish head, the canyon wren is well adapted for probing for spiders and insects in the crevices of boulders. Canyon wrens move about nimbly, climbing upward as well as downward on steep-sided, nearly vertical rock faces. They nest in sheltered areas among the rocks, which provide protective shade and cooler temperatures during periods of intense heat. They have rusty-brown upperparts, a white upper breast, and a chestnut-colored belly. Their bright rusty tails are barred with black.

Bewick's Wren

Thryomanes bewickii

SPANISH: *Saltapared de Bewick, Chivirín cola oscura, Troglodita colinegro*

FAMILY: Wrens–Troglodytidae

LENGTH & WINGSPAN: 5¼ inches; 7 inches

Pronounced like "Buick," this wren was named after Thomas Bewick, an English artist and wood engraver who was a friend of John James Audubon. Bewick's wren is widespread and common in many parts of the Southwest. It is an active and curious bird, investigating and probing among crevices in tree branches, trunks, and brush piles for insects, their larvae and eggs, and small invertebrates. It generally keeps to cover, making quick, short flights to the next tree or brush pile. Light-colored below, Bewick's wrens have brownish-gray upperparts and a distinct white line above the eye. Their long tails, which they characteristically wag from side to side, are edged with white spots. These wrens are quite vocal, with a number of variable songs.

Ruby-crowned Kinglet

Regulus calendula

SPANISH: *Reyezuelo de corona roja, Reyezuelo de rojo, Reyezuelo monicolorado*

FAMILY: Kinglets–Regulidae

LENGTH & WINGSPAN: 4¼ inches; 7½ inches

This extremely active little bird is one of North America's smallest songbirds, and it is a common winter visitor in the lowlands of the Southwest. During the breeding season, it moves up

in elevation to nest in areas of coniferous forest. Kinglets seem to be constantly on the move, flicking their wings slightly open and moving quickly through the vegetation in pursuit of insects. This nervous twitching gives them a hyperactive look, and their short, chattering call notes seem to complete the profile. Rather nondescript-looking otherwise, they have olive-gray upperparts with two white wing bars and a ring of white around the eye that gives them a big-eyed or surprised appearance. The male has red crown feathers that are visible only when he raises them in response to a potential mate, rival, or predator. Ruby-crowned kinglets are unusual in that the females may lay up to a dozen eggs, the largest clutch size of any North American songbird.

Black-tailed Gnatcatcher

Polioptila melanura
SPANISH: *Perlita del desierto, Perlita colinegra, Pisita colinegra*
FAMILY: Old World Warblers and Gnatcatchers–Sylviidae
LENGTH & WINGSPAN: 4½ inches; 5½ inches

Gnatcatchers are small and slim, long-tailed birds that flit actively about in shrubs and trees, searching for insects. There are several species, but the black-tailed gnatcatcher is the one adapted to the desert Southwest. Pairs remain together all year long and stay in contact by a variety of buzzy-sounding call notes. Both sexes are blue-gray above and whitish below, and have long black-and-white tails. During breeding season, the males are adorned with black caps. Breeding pairs are often parasitized by cowbirds.

Delinquent nesters themselves, adult cowbirds lay their eggs in other birds' nests. The unsuspecting hosts incubate and feed the young cowbirds as if they were their own offspring. Since the cowbird babies tend to be much larger than the young gnatcatchers, it is only the young cowbirds that survive.

Western Bluebird

Sialia mexicana

SPANISH: *Azulejo de garanta azul, Azulejo gorjiazul*

FAMILY: Thrushes–Turdidae

LENGTH & WINGSPAN: 7 inches; 13½ inches

Bluebirds are among the most popular of North American birds. Males are azure blue with bright, rusty-orange breasts. In winter, small flocks are often seen at lower elevations, feeding on the berries of mistletoe and juniper. In summer, bluebirds frequent open mountain meadows, where they feed mainly on insects. They are typically seen perching on a fence post or tree limb and then fluttering to the ground to snatch an insect from the grass. They sometimes hover briefly in midair before dropping to the ground. Bluebirds nest in holes and use natural cavities in trees or old woodpecker holes. Within the cavity, they build a loose cup of twigs and weeds. Bluebird numbers have declined in recent years due to the loss of natural nest sites and competition with other cavity-nesting birds.

Hermit Thrush

Catharus guttatus

SPANISH: *Zorzal de cola rufa, Zorzalito colirrufo*

FAMILY: Thrushes–Turdidae

LENGTH & WINGSPAN: 6¾ inches; 11½ inches

Hermit thrushes are quiet, secretive birds that live in forested areas. They spend most of their time on the ground, plucking insects from leaf litter or the soil. They characteristically hop or run short distances on the ground, then stop abruptly and peer

about from an upright posture. While pausing, they often raise their tails up quickly and down slowly, and give a soft *"chuck"* call. Hermit thrushes also hover briefly at shrubs and trees to garner fruits or berries. They have soft colors: brown above and spotted below with reddish brown on the tail. During the breeding season, their melodious, flute-like songs with bell-like tones may be heard throughout the forest.

American Robin

Turdus migratorius
SPANISH: *Mirlo primavera, Zorzal pechirrojo*
FAMILY: Thrushes–Turdidae
LENGTH & WINGSPAN: 10 inches; 17 inches

One of the first birds that every school-child learns is the American robin, the most widespread member of the thrush family in North America. Robins have dark rusty breasts, gray backs, white throats decorated with dark stripes, and yellow bills. In the Southwest, they are found most often at high elevations, where they are generally seen on the ground, running with short, straight dashes, and pausing frequently to scan for food. During the spring and summer months, they consume earthworms and other ground-dwelling invertebrates; in fall and winter, they feed mainly on fruit. During some winters when the food crop has failed elsewhere, robins may "invade" lowland areas, where they feed on common backyard plants like pyracantha.

Northern Mockingbird

Mimus polyglottos
SPANISH: *Cenzontle norteño, Cenzontle, Jilguero ruiseñor*
FAMILY: Mockingbirds and Thrashers–Mimidae
LENGTH & WINGSPAN: 10 inches; 14 inches

These slim, long-tailed members of the mimic-thrush family have impressive voices. Mockingbirds mimic the songs of other birds, as well as other nonavian and mechanical sounds. A male's repertoire may contain more than 150 distinct song types, and these change during the course of its lifetime. Males sing to defend territory and to attract mates, often in the middle of the night. When walking or running on the ground, mockingbirds frequently raise their wings in several jerky movements, exposing their conspicuous white wing patches. They may also unexpectedly leap up into the air. The function of these behavior patterns is unknown, but there is speculation that it may be a way of startling insects or potential predators, or it may be a territorial display. Mockingbirds consume insects as well as fruit. They are permanent residents in a variety of open habitats throughout the Southwestern lowlands.

Curve-billed Thrasher

Toxostoma curvirostre
SPANISH: *Cuitlacoche de pico curvo*
FAMILY: Mockingbirds and Thrashers–Mimidae
LENGTH & WINGSPAN: 11 inches; 13½ inches

The strident *"whit wheet"* of the curve-billed thrasher is a familiar sound in arid lands of the Southwest. This bird is in the same family as the northern mockingbird

and is quite a songster as well. Its rich, warbling notes are similar to the mockingbird's, but are less repetitive and include fewer imitations. Almost uniformly brown with some mottling on the chest, the curve-billed thrasher has yellow-orange eyes that give it a rather startled look, and a downward-curving bill. This bird spends a great deal of time on the ground, sweeping its heavy bill from side to side in the leaf litter or soil, searching for grubs and insects. When digging in very hard, compacted soil, it sometimes braces its tail against the ground and pounds straight down with heavy blows of the bill. This species is remarkably specialized in its choice of nesting sites, almost always selecting cholla cacti. The spines of the cactus may help to protect the nest from snakes and other predators. Cactus spines that interfere with the nests are broken off. Holding the offending spine in its bill, the thrasher twists its head vigorously until the spine is severed.

Phainopepla

Phainopepla nitens
SPANISH: *Capulinero negro, Tohuehui*
FAMILY: Silky-flycatchers–Ptilogonatidae
LENGTH & WINGSPAN: 7¾ inches; 11 inches

Phainopeplas belong to the silky-flycatcher family, a name referring to their soft, sleek feathers and their agility in catching insects on the wing. The male's shimmering black plumage inspired the Greek name *phainopepla,* which means "shining robe." Females are charcoal-gray in color, and both sexes have white wing patches (mainly visible in flight), long tails, slender crests, and red eyes. They are common in the Sonoran Desert, where they are associated with mistletoe. During the winter, they depend upon mistletoe fruit for food and are largely responsible for its spread. The seeds are dispersed as birds move from tree to tree, carrying the seeds on their bills or feet, or depositing them after passage through the digestive tract. Phainopeplas also consume insects. They have a buoyant and often zigzagging flight pattern, changing directions erratically as they pursue insects in the air. There is some thought that these birds may breed in two distinct habitats at different times of year—an unusual pattern among North American songbirds. From February to April they breed in the Sonoran Desert of Arizona and the Colorado Desert of California. As the summer heat intensifies and berry supplies dwindle, the birds leave the desert and move to oak and sycamore canyons, where they are thought to breed a second time.

Female

Olive Warbler

Peucedramus taeniatus
SPANISH: *Ocotero enmascarado*
FAMILY: Olive Warbler–Peucedramidae
LENGTH & WINGSPAN: 5¼ inches; 9¼ inches

The genus name *Peucedramus* is from the Greek *peuce,* meaning "pine," and *dram(ema),* which means "running." This "runner in the pines" is a breeding bird in open forests in southeastern Arizona and southwest New Mexico at elevations of 8,500–12,000 feet. Generally found high in the pine forest canopy, olive warblers give good meaning to the term "warbler neck" for those birdwatchers trying to catch a glimpse of this bird. Although similar in appearance to wood-warblers, olive warblers were recently placed in their own family due to some apparent differences: flared and notched tails, long thin bills, and soft whistled calls. These birds sometimes travel in mixed flocks—often with nuthatches, chickadees, and brown creepers—as they forage for insects to eat.

Male olive warbler

Adult males display distinctive coppery-orange heads and sides to the neck accentuated by dark masks. Females show more subtle facial masks and are tinted with buffy yellow on the head and neck. Cup-shaped nests are built by females, and are often strategically veiled by bundles of pine needles.

Lucy's Warbler

Vermivora luciae
SPANISH: *Chipe de rabadilla rufa, Gusanero de Lucy*
FAMILY: Wood-warblers–Parulidae
LENGTH & WINGSPAN: 4¼ inches; 7 inches

Lucy's warbler is a small, rather inconspicuous bird of desert streamside habitats. Dull gray in color, it has a white ring around a beady dark eye, a chestnut-colored rump patch, and a small patch of chestnut on the crown. The latter is rarely seen, except when the bird is excited. Lucy's warbler is unusual in that it nests in cavities—one of only two North American warblers that does so. Nests usually are located behind the loose bark of a tree, in a natural cavity, or old woodpecker hole, and are well woven with twigs, leaves, and mesquite leaf stems. Lucy's warbler, sometimes referred to as the desert warbler, breeds in the southwestern U.S. and winters in western Mexico.

Yellow-rumped Warbler

Dendroica coronata
SPANISH: *Chipe de rabadilla amarilla, Chipe coronada, Chipe grupidorado común*
FAMILY: Wood-warblers–Parulidae
LENGTH & WINGSPAN: 5½ inches; 9¼ inches

Versatile in their feeding habits, yellow-rumped warblers may search among twigs and leaves for insects, hover while taking insects from foliage, or fly out to catch flying insects in midair. Unlike most warblers, they also eat berries. Yellow-rumps nest in coniferous and mixed forests. During the winter, they move to lower elevations in response to colder weather and a decline in the abundance of insects. They look rather dull in their more subtle winter plumage, but they still have the trademark yellow rump patch. The western form of yellow-rumped warbler, with its yellow throat, is also known as Audubon's warbler. In the Southwest, this is the warbler most likely to be seen.

Black-throated Gray Warbler

Dendroica nigrescens
SPANISH: *Chipe negrogris*
FAMILY: Wood-warblers–Parulidae
LENGTH & WINGSPAN: 5 inches; 7 ¾ inches

Black-throated gray warblers breed in the southwestern U.S. and are common in spring and summer in dry oak, piñon, and juniper woodlands. For their nests, they construct a deep cup on a horizontal branch using pieces of bark, weeds, and grass, and often line it with feathers. These handsome warblers are black, white, and gray with strong face patterns and tiny, bright yellow spots in front of their eyes, though the latter are often difficult to see. Males sport black throats and bibs. They move methodically among the foliage, sometimes hovering at leaves to pick off insects. Most individuals depart late in the fall to spend the winter in Mexico, but some individuals may remain. During the winter and when migrating they are often found in mixed-species flocks.

Wilson's Warbler
Wilsonia pusilla
SPANISH: *Chipe de corona negra*
FAMILY: Wood-warblers–Parulidae
LENGTH & WINGSPAN: 4¾ inches; 7 inches

Naturalist Alexander Wilson, a pioneer American ornithologist of the late-eighteenth and early-nineteenth centuries, was the first to describe this warbler that bears his name. This small, golden-yellow bird is a migrant through the Southwest in late spring and may be found in hot lowland thickets and along wooded streams. It typically feeds within ten feet of the ground, actively moving through bushes and trees in pursuit of insects, and is sometimes difficult to see because of its skittish nature. Wilson's warbler has a dark, beady eye that stands out conspicuously against its bright yellow face. The bird originally was called pileolated warbler, a reference to the male's distinctive round black cap. In recent years populations have declined in the West, probably due to the destruction of riparian habitats.

Red-faced Warbler

Cardellina rubrifrons
SPANISH: *Chipe de cara roja*
FAMILY: Wood-warblers–Parulidae
LENGTH & WINGSPAN: 5½ inches;
8½ inches

A swath of black, worn like a scarf, adorns the head of this bird and is striking against the bright carmine-red on the face and throat. Sexes are similar. These unmistakable birds are locally common during the summer months in montane forests of Arizona and New Mexico at elevations of 6,500–9,000 feet, where they live among ponderosa pine, Engelmann's spruce, and Douglas fir, as well as in thickets of aspen and oak. They spend much of their time foraging for caterpillars and leafhoppers on the outer edges of various conifer trees, but will also fly out to snag small flies and other airborne insects. Unlike most other wood-warblers, these brightly colored birds nest on the ground, scratching out shallow scrapes among fallen leaves. Nest depressions are usually concealed by rocks, logs, or a clump of grass. The word "warble" means to sing sweetly, and the red-faced warbler does just that.

Painted Redstart

Myioborus pictus
SPANISH: *Pavito de ala blanca*
FAMILY: Wood-warblers–Parulidae
LENGTH & WINGSPAN: 5¾ inches;
8¼ inches

Painted redstarts are elegant members of the warbler family. Both sexes have black heads and upperparts, and vivid crimson-colored lower breasts. Partial white rings around the lower portion of the eyes give them a sleepy-eyed appearance. Painted

redstarts are southwestern U.S. specialties and are found in oak canyons and pine-oak forests in southern Arizona, southwest New Mexico, and Texas. They frequently are seen clambering up and down tree trunks in search of insects. As they climb about the sides of the trunk, they often expressively fan their tails, showing off white outer tail feathers. These redstarts usually nest on the ground, typically on a bank or rocky hillside not far from a stream. Their distinctive song sounds like *"weeta, weeta, weeta."*

Hepatic Tanager
Piranga flava
SPANISH: *Tangara encinera*
FAMILY: Tanagers–Thraupidae
LENGTH & WINGSPAN: 8 inches; 12½ inches

Tanagers are tree-dwelling, medium-sized birds with stout bills, and are often brightly colored. The male hepatic tanager is brick-red in color, with a dusky cheek patch and a gray bill. Females display the shadowy cheek patch as well, with dull yellow on the throat and forehead. During the spring and summer months, hepatic tanagers live in pine–oak woodlands in Arizona, New Mexico, and Texas. They move slowly, rather high in the canopy, in quest of caterpillars and beetles, but also fly out to catch insects in midair. As the breeding season progresses, they may feast on the fruits of wild grapes as well. The male delivers a loud clear warbling song from atop a tall tree to attract a mate. For its nest, the hepatic tanager engineers a saucer-shaped cup made from grasses and various plant parts—generally in a conifer, oak, or sometimes a sycamore tree. This bird winters from northern Mexico to northern Nicaragua.

Summer Tanager

Piranga rubra
SPANISH: *Tángara roja, Cardenal veranero, Tángara de paso*
FAMILY: Tanagers–Thraupidae
LENGTH & WINGSPAN: 7¾ inches; 12 inches

Male summer tanagers are a striking rose-red, and females are yellowish-green. Both sexes have light-colored bills. These birds move rather deliberately through the trees, pausing to look about for insects or fruits. They are noted for their consumption of bees and wasps, both in the adult and larval stages, and have been observed foraging at wasp nests. They are able to remove a bee's or wasp's stinger by wiping it on a tree branch prior to consumption. The snappy *"pit-i-tuck"* call of the summer tanager is a characteristic sound of riparian woodlands in the spring and summer. In the fall, they travel to central Mexico and as far south as northern South America to spend the winter.

Western Tanager

Piranga ludoviciana
SPANISH: *Tángara de capucha roja, Tángara aliblanca migratoria*
FAMILY: Tanagers–Thraupidae
LENGTH & WINGSPAN: 7¼ inches; 11½ inches

With their brilliant yellow-and-black bodies and radiant red-orange heads, male western tanagers are among the most beautiful of birds. They breed at high elevations in the Southwest in open coniferous and mixed coniferous-deciduous forests. During migration, large numbers may appear in almost any habitat, including grassland, desert, and city parks and gardens. Rather sluggish in behavior, they move about through the vegetation while reaching to pick insects from the foliage. During the breeding season they feed mainly on insects, but at other times of year fruit and berries constitute an important part of their diet. Western tanagers winter in Mexico and Central America.

Canyon Towhee
Pipilo fuscus
SPANISH: *Rascador pardo, Vieja*
FAMILY: Sparrows and Towhees–
Emberizidae
LENGTH & WINGSPAN: 9 inches;
11½ inches

Canyon towhees are stout, mostly brown birds with longish tails. Under the base of the tail there is a patch of rusty brown. Never far from cover, these large sparrows venture out to feed on open ground, but then fly back to dense bushes when alarmed. When agitated or excited, they often raise the feathers on the head, which gives them a slightly crested appearance. Canyon towhees are usually seen in mated pairs, and hunt for food on the ground by using a double scratching motion with both feet. They eat mostly seeds, but in the summer consume many insects. Canyon towhees tend to remain in one area, rarely moving even a short distance from their nesting areas. They may be found along dry waterways in lower deserts, in upland desert scrub, and up into the edges of pine–oak woodland.

Abert's Towhee
Pipilo aberti
SPANISH: *Rascador de Abert*
FAMILY: Sparrows and
Towhees–Emberizidae
LENGTH & WINGSPAN: 9½
inches; 11 inches

The genus name *Pipilo* is from the Latin *pico*, which means to "chirp" or "peep." Abert's towhee makes a high-pitched *"teek"* call, which is often followed by an assortment of

harsh, jumbling notes. These ground-dwelling skulkers are brown in color with black masks that set off their pale bills. They advertise a patch of reddish-brown under their long tails, which they often elevate as they scurry along the ground. Males and females are identical in appearance. Like other towhees, these birds are known for using the motion of their feet to stir up insects and seeds to eat. Abert's towhee is a common resident in areas of dense brush along waterways in the Southwest, but also lives in gardens in some low-elevation cities such as Phoenix, Yuma, and Tucson. The bird was named after U.S. Army major James W. Abert, who collected the first known-to-science specimen in New Mexico.

Rufous-winged Sparrow

Aimophila carpalis
SPANISH: *Zacatonero de ala rufa*
FAMILY: Sparrows and Towhees–Emberizidae
LENGTH & WINGSPAN: 5¾ inches; 7½ inches

This uncommon and much-sought-after species is a year-round resident in south-central Arizona, where it frequents low-elevation grasslands sprinkled with mesquite trees. Rufous-winged sparrows are elusive because they spend so much time lurking in dense grass. During the summer rainy season males perch on high to sing and advertise for mates, making them much more visible. Named for their reddish-

brown wings, both sexes have unmarked gray breasts, finely streaked backs, and rufous-colored crown stripes. These resourceful birds feed on ants, caterpillars, and grasshoppers during certain seasons and then consume the seeds of grasses and weeds and the fruits of desert hackberry at other times of year. They are equally flexible in terms of their breeding habits and do not attempt to reproduce every single year. Nesting is most favorable in years following heavy winter or summer rains when adequate seed supplies are ensured for feeding the young.

Brewer's Sparrow
Spizella breweri
SPANISH: *Gorrión de Brewer, Chimbito de Brewer, Gorrión indefinido desértico*
FAMILY: Sparrows and Towhees–Emberizidae
LENGTH & WINGSPAN: 5½ inches; 7½ inches

Brewer's sparrow was named after Thomas M. Brewer, a prominent ornithologist of the mid-1800s who was noted for his studies of birds' eggs. Brewer's sparrows are small birds with long tails, and they have subtle, muted colors and markings that blend in well with their typical habitat, sagebrush scrub. Most individuals breed in and around the Great Basin. In winter months, they fly southward to the Sonoran and Chihuahuan deserts of the Southwest, where they may be seen in flocks often numbering in the hundreds, hopping on the ground or among the branches of shrubs, feeding on seeds. Their song is a series of ascending and descending buzzy trills. Brewer's sparrows are able to exist for long periods of time without water and probably eat insects year-round to help maintain their water balance.

Black-throated Sparrow
Amphispiza bilineata
SPANISH: *Gorrión de garganta negra, Gorrión gorjinegro carirrayado*
FAMILY: Sparrows and Towhees–Emberizidae
LENGTH & WINGSPAN: 5½ inches; 7¾ inches

Smartly patterned for a sparrow, adult birds are gray with a distinctive black-and-white face pattern. Black-throated sparrows have pronounced white lines above the eyes, white whisker stripes, and black throats that extend down onto the chest. They are very common in some parts of the Southwest and live in a variety of habitats, but are most common in deserts, from barren creosote-and-saltbush flats to the richly vegetated Sonoran Desert. They are able to survive without water for long periods of time, obtaining moisture from the insects and plants that they eat. They form small flocks during the wintertime and may be seen feeding on the ground in open areas, often vocalizing with a tinkling call. Black-throated sparrows nest on or near the ground in small bushes.

White-crowned Sparrow
Zonotrichia leucophrys
SPANISH: *Gorrión de corona blanca, Zacatero mixto, Gorrión gorriblanco*
FAMILY: Sparrows and Towhees–Emberizidae
LENGTH & WINGSPAN: 7 inches; 9½ inches

White-crowned sparrows are widespread winter visitors to the Southwest. Adults have pinkish bills and puffy crowns with black-and-white stripes. They often raise and lower the feathers on their heads in response to excitement, aggression, or danger, giving the head a tufted appearance. White-crowns may be found in many different habitats, including along roadsides, in grassland and riparian areas, and in cities. During the winter, they are usually in small flocks and spend a lot of time on the ground, rummaging for grass and weed seeds. White-crowns often perform a double scratching motion with their feet, hoping to uncover some food morsel from the leaf litter or soil. At other times of year, they feed on flowers, berries, small fruits, insects, and spiders. Their song is a distinctive, plaintive whistle followed by a series of trills. They often flock with other sparrow species and are seldom far from cover.

Northern Cardinal

Cardinalis cardinalis
SPANISH: *Cardenal norteño, Cardenal rojo*
FAMILY: Cardinals, Grosbeaks, and Buntings–
Cardinalidae
LENGTH & WINGSPAN: 8¾ inches; 12 inches

Perhaps no other North American bird is so commonly illustrated as the northern cardinal. One of the first birds that we all seem to draw or color in elementary school is that brilliant red bird with the jaunty crest. Reasons for the

Male

popularity of this species are undoubtedly its dazzling color, its distinctive shape, and the ease with which males can be identified. The male cardinal is brilliant red all over with a black face, a large pinkish-orange bill, and a pointed crest. The female has the

same brightly colored bill, but her feathers are mostly buffy brown. Their heavy bills are adapted for extracting seeds from plants and flowers by cutting or crushing the shells. Locally common in the desert Southwest, cardinals are found in Arizona, a few areas in New Mexico, and west Texas, often in desert washes and streamside thickets. They feed mostly while hopping on the ground, searching for seeds, insects, and berries. They have a musical, whistled song that sounds like *"what cheer what cheer cheer."* Males sing year-round, and females also sing on occasion.

Female

Pyrrhuloxia

Cardinalis sinuatus

SPANISH: *Cardenal desértico, Cardenal torito, Cardenal pardo, Cardenal gris*

FAMILY: Cardinals, Grosbeaks, and Buntings–Cardinalidae

LENGTH & WINGSPAN: 8¾ inches; 12 inches

Female

Pyrrhuloxias are found in Arizona, New Mexico, Texas, and south into Mexico. They seem to tolerate drier and more open habitat than cardinals, frequenting lower stretches of arid canyons, mesquite desert, and thorn scrub. The male is gray, washed with red, and both sexes have wispy crests. Their stubby yellow bills are shaped more like those of parrots, in contrast to the pink, triangular bill of the cardinal. In fall and winter, pyrrhuloxias often hunt for food in loose flocks. They are opportunistic feeders, eating beetles, caterpillars, grasshoppers, seeds, and berries. They often consume cactus fruit and seem to be particularly fond of the fruits of desert Christmas cholla. They are undoubtedly

Male

dependent upon insect food and fruit for much of their water requirement. Pyrrhulox-ias typically fly short distances between perches with a few wingbeats and then a glide.

Black-headed Grosbeak

Pheucticus melanocephalus

SPANISH: *Picogordo tigrillo, Frío, Picogrueso pechicafé*

FAMILY: Cardinals, Grosbeaks, and Buntings–Cardinalidae

LENGTH & WINGSPAN: 8¼ inches; 12½ inches

Black-headed grosbeaks are medium-sized finches with rich, melodious songs. Adult males are smartly patterned with black, white, and orange feathers and have large conical bills. Females are more subtly patterned with buff and brown. In the springtime, black-headed grosbeaks arrive in the U.S. to breed. They may be found in a variety of habitats, including cottonwood and willow groves in the desert; canyons of piñon, juniper, and oak; and even mountain valleys with mature pines and aspen groves. Both sexes sing, often from the nest, apparently as a means of communication. For the winter, black-headed grosbeaks return to Mexico, where they are known to eat large numbers of monarch butterflies. They are one of the few birds able to eat monarchs despite the noxious chemical these butterflies produce from eating milkweeds during their larval stage.

Blue Grosbeak

Passerina caerulea

SPANISH: *Picogordo azul*

FAMILY: Cardinals, Grosbeaks, and Buntings–Cardinalidae

LENGTH & WINGSPAN: 6¾ inches; 11 inches

Blue grosbeaks are adaptable birds, occurring across much of the southern half of North America during the breeding season. In the Southwest they are denizens of streamside

Female

Male blue grosbeak

thickets and mesquite groves, where they are often difficult to see since they haunt low weedy patches. They forage for food on or near the ground, seeking out succulent caterpillars and cutworms, grasshoppers, spiders, and cicadas. They also harvest weed and grain seeds as well as the fruits of some wild plants. The "gros" in the "beak" refers to the size of their large, conical-shaped bills. Females are generally on the drab side— mostly brown—but male blue grosbeaks are real lookers, extremely striking in shades of deep indigo blue accented with rusty-colored wing bars. The male sings from atop a tall weed or bush to attract a mate. The nest is built by the female and is a compact open cup made of twigs, weeds, roots, leaves, bark, and sometimes cast-off snakeskins.

Varied Bunting

Passerina versicolor
SPANISH: *Colorín morado*
FAMILY: Cardinals, Grosbeaks, and
Buntings–Cardinalidae
LENGTH & WINGSPAN: 5½ inches; 7¾
inches

At first glance, the male of this species appears dark all over, but when the light hits his feathers just right he is absolutely stunning—dipped in shades of red, purple, blue, and brown. The Latin species

Female

name *versicolor* is perfect, for it means "variegated" or "of various colors." The female varied bunting is a lackluster brown but shows a hint of blue in the wings and tail. These shy, uncommon birds prefer brushy territory near the Mexican border for their late-summer breeding season, often frequenting areas of thick mesquite along desert washes. Varied buntings build cup-shaped nests in the crotch of a bush or low tree, and nest materials include dry weeds,

Male varied bunting

plant stems, grasses, and cotton, as well as cast-off snakeskins. The dietary preferences of these birds are not well-studied, but they probably feed on insects and seeds, as well as on some berries.

Female

Red-winged Blackbird

Agelaius phoeniceus

SPANISH: *Tordo sargento, Tordo alirrojo, Tordo capitán*

FAMILY: Blackbirds–Icteridae

LENGTH & WINGSPAN: 8¾ inches; 13 inches

Red-winged blackbirds were named for the males' red shoulder epaulets. Much of the time, the scarlet is concealed and only the yellowish margins of the shoulder patch shows. Otherwise, the males are completely black. Female birds are less boldly marked and are streaked with brown. During nonbreeding season, red-winged blackbirds are quite gregarious and travel and roost

Male red-winged blackbird

in flocks. They often are seen walking on the ground, looking for insects and seeds. In spring and summer, their chorus of liquid gurgling is a distinctive sound around fresh-water marshes, roadside ditches, and pasturelands. Red-winged blackbirds usually nest among reed stalks, cattails, or bulrushes, weaving their nests of plant material and lining the inner cup with mud.

Eastern Meadowlark
Sturnella magna
SPANISH: *Pradero tortilla con chile*
FAMILY: Blackbirds–Icteridae
LENGTH & WINGSPAN: 9½ inches; 14 inches

Western Meadowlark
Sturnella neglecta
SPANISH: *Pradero occidental*
FAMILY: Blackbirds–Icteridae
LENGTH & WINGSPAN: 9½ inches; 14½ inches

Western meadowlark, with its elegant yellow breast with a black "V" pattern, is a bird of grassy country and cultivated fields. It spends a great deal of time walking on the ground, often overturning dirt clods to look for insects and seeds. In winter, these birds usually are found in good-sized flocks. When they fly, they beat their wings rapidly several times and then alternate with short glides. Their voice is double-noted and flute-like. The ranges of eastern and western meadowlark overlap in central and southeastern Arizona, central New Mexico, and southwest Texas. Although the colors and pattern of the two birds are very similar, the easiest way to tell them apart is by their very different voices. Eastern meadowlark's song is a series of clear whistles, unlike the rapid, complex bubbling of its western cousin. Eastern meadowlarks, seldom seen in large flocks, seem to prefer natural grassland rather than the agricultural country and desert farm fields that attract western meadowlarks.

Eastern meadowlark

Yellow-headed Blackbird

Xanthocephalus xanthocephalus

SPANISH: *Tordo de cabeza amarilla*

FAMILY: Blackbirds–Icteridae

LENGTH & WINGSPAN: 9½ inches; 15 inches

The scientific name *Xanthocephalus* means "yellow head," which is appropriate for the male of this species. With their jet-black bodies, saffron-yellow heads, and white wing patches, flocks of these highly social birds are a striking sight. During the winter, they migrate to the southern U.S. and Mexico, and may be found around freshwater marshes, wetlands, or open agricultural areas. They are sometimes seen following farm

Yellow-headed blackbird

machinery in fields, feeding on whatever insects or seeds are turned up by the plow. Their hoarse, rasping voices sound a bit like rusty hinges. In spring, they move to marshes to the north, where they nest among the cattails in noisy colonies. Their nests are interwoven networks of wet vegetation firmly lashed to reeds, cattails, or bulrushes in standing water.

Great-tailed Grackle

Quiscalus mexicanus
SPANISH: *Zanate mexicano*
FAMILY: Blackbirds–Icteridae
LENGTH & WINGSPAN: 15–18 inches; 19–23 inches

Great-tailed grackles are large, conspicuous blackbirds with oversized tails. The males' feathers have a purplish sheen, and their yellow eyes contrast sharply. Males are even more conspicuous when courting the smaller, brownish females. Fluffing out their feathers, they spread

Female

their large tails and rapidly flutter their wings as they strut around the female bird. At the same time, they make a series of harsh call notes and may posture with their bills pointing straight up in the air. Omnivorous in their feeding habits, great-tailed grackles can live in a variety of habitats and have expanded their range in the last several decades. Their shrill, discordant notes, whistles, and clucks are a familiar sound in city parks of the Southwest. When not in breeding season, grackles roost communally at night.

Male great-tailed grackle

Hooded Oriole

Icterus cucullatus
SPANISH: *Bolsero enmascarado, Bolsero cuculado*
FAMILY: Blackbirds–Icteridae
LENGTH & WINGSPAN: 8 inches; 10½ inches

Hooded oriole is a slim, brilliantly colored member of the blackbird family and is found from the southwestern U.S. to southern Mexico. The male's head and underparts are a bright

yellow-orange, offset by a black back, tail, and throat. The female is more subtly colored, with an olive-gray back and greenish-yellow underparts. Hooded orioles have several distinctive vocalizations, including a soft *"wink"* call note, and a dry, chattering rattle. They often nest in palm trees, where they weave a pouch of grass or shredded palm fibers through overhanging leaves. Hooded orioles eat insects, berries, and nectar, and are regular visitors to hummingbird feeders. They forage for food among vegetation in a somewhat slow and deliberate manner, and also probe into flowers for nectar.

Scott's Oriole

Icterus parisorum
SPANISH: *Bolsero tunero, Bolsero parisino*
FAMILY: Blackbirds–Icteridae
LENGTH & WINGSPAN: 9 inches; 12½ inches

Scott's oriole is another vividly colored member of the blackbird family. The rich lemon-yellow underparts of the male contrast strikingly with his solid black head and back. This bird migrates to the Southwest in March or April to breed. Its impressive nest is a hanging woven basket, often placed in a yucca plant. The long yucca fibers are often used to weave the nest. Scott's oriole lives in a variety of habitats, from dense oak woods of lower canyons to open grassland with scattered yuccas, but it tends to avoid true desert areas. Its song is a series of rich, melodious whistles. A very early fall migrant, this bird departs for Mexico in July or August, although some individuals may spend the winter in southern Arizona and southern California. Primarily an insect eater, Scott's orioles also regularly visit flowers for nectar.

House Finch

Carpodacus mexicanus
SPANISH: *Pinzón mexicano, Gorrión doméstico, Gorrión común, Gorrión mexicano*
FAMILY: Finches–Fringillidae
LENGTH & WINGSPAN: 6 inches; 9½ inches

House finches are common at all seasons from the center of cities to remote desert canyons. Originally native to the Southwest, house finches have expanded their range in recent years.

Male

Female house finch

In the 1940s, pet shops in New York City were illegally selling these birds as "Holly-wood Finches." Threatened with legal action, some shop owners released their birds—which survived and began to colonize the New York suburbs. Proving themselves remarkably adaptable, the finches rapidly spread to occupy most of eastern North America, and eastern populations have met western populations on the Great Plains. House finches are streaky brown, and males are decorated with accents of red. These are social birds with cheery songs and usually are found in small groups. In addition to seeds, house finches also feed on fruit, flower buds, and a few insects. They often are seen visiting hummingbird feeders for sugar water.

Lesser Goldfinch
Carduelis psaltria
SPANISH: *Dominico de dorso oscuro, Jilguero dominico*
FAMILY: Finches–Fringillidae
LENGTH & WINGSPAN: 4½ inches; 8 inches

Lesser goldfinches are small, sociable birds that feed primarily on the seeds of weeds and other plants. They forage among branches actively and acrobatically, some-times hanging upside down to reach into a seed head. They also may eat flower buds, fruits, and occasionally tiny insects. Males have bright yellow underparts and black

Male lesser goldfinch

caps, and the back may be either greenish or black. The males have been found to incorporate the songs of other bird species into their repertoires, and their mimicry seems to vary geographically. Goldfinches have an undulating flight pattern, dipping up and down as they fly. They are found in open country with scattered trees and are often nomadic and sporadic in occurrence, roaming around in search of areas with the best food source.

Female lesser goldfinch

ADDITIONAL READING

· · · · · ·

Ehrlich, Paul R., David S. Dobkin, and Darryl Wheye. *The Birder's Handbook: A Field Guide to the Natural History of North American Birds.* New York: Simon and Schuster, 1988.

Elphick, Chris, John B. Dunning Jr., and David Allen Sibley (eds.). *The Sibley Guide to Bird Life and Behavior.* New York: Alfred A. Knopf, 2001.

Kaufman, Kenn. *Birds of North America.* Kaufman Focus Guides. Boston, Massachusetts: Houghton Mifflin Company, 2000.

Peterson, Roger Tory. *Peterson Field Guide to Birds of North America.* Boston, Massachusetts: Houghton Mifflin Company, 2008.

Sibley, David Allen. *The Sibley Field Guide to Birds of Western North America.* New York: Alfred A. Knopf, 2003.

INDEX OF FEATURED SPECIES

• • • • • •

Rio Nuevo Publishers
P.O. Box 5250
Tucson, AZ 85703-0250
www.rionuevo.com

Shown on the front cover (clockwise from top): Sandhill Crane, White-winged Dove, Black-bellied Whistling-Duck, Brown-crested Flycatcher. On page 2: White-winged Dove; page 4: Northern Cardinal; page 5: American Kestrel; page 90: Cooper's Hawk; page 93: Costa's Hummingbird; page 94: Gila Woodpecker.

Library of Congress Cataloging-in-Publication Data

Hassler, Lynn.
Birds of the American Southwest / Lynn Hassler. — Expanded 2nd ed.
    p. cm. — (Wild west series)
Includes bibliographical references.
ISBN-13: 978-1-933855-33-2 (pbk. : alk. paper)
ISBN-10: 1-933855-33-9 (pbk. : alk. paper) 1. Birds—Mexico—Identification. 2. Birds—Southwest, New—Identification. 3. Birds—Southwest, New—Pictorial works. 4. Birds—Mexico—
Pictorial works. I. Title.
QL683.S75K38 2008
598.0979—dc22

                          2008025411

Printed in Canada.
Book Design: Karen Schober, Seattle, Washington

10 9 8 7 6 5 4 3 2 1